Supply Chain Resilience

Supply Chain Resilience

Survival Strategies for Turbulent Times

Andreas Karaoulanis

BEP

BUSINESS EXPERT PRESS

Leader in applied, concise business books

First published in 2025 by
Business Expert Press, LLC
222 East 46th Street, New York, NY 10017
www.businessexpertpress.com

ISBN-13: 978-1-63742-778-1 (paperback)
ISBN-13: 978-1-63742-779-8 (ebook)

Business Expert Press Supply and Operations Management Collection

First edition: 2025

10 9 8 7 6 5 4 3 2 1

EU SAFETY REPRESENTATIVE
Mare Nostrum Group B.V.
Mauritskade 21D
1091 GC Amsterdam
The Netherlands
gpsr@mare-nostrum.co.uk

Description

In a world where pandemics, natural disasters, climate change, and wars are only some of the disruptions that supply chains are facing, resiliency has become the alpha and the omega of supply chain management.

This book navigates us through thick and thin and gives us a holistic description of what is supply chain resilience, which are the factors that affect it, and which are the most effective resilience strategies that we need to implement in our supply chains in order to survive during turbulent times.

The book is divided into three distinct parts. In the first part, one discusses the term supply chain resilience—its importance, its components, and the most important supply chain resilience metrics. The author presents real-life examples of well-known companies that were successful in enhancing the resilience of their supply chains. The second part presents all the factors that can influence the resilience of a supply chain and concludes with discussions of 17 supply chain resilience strategies, which can be used by almost any company, in any industry, in any part of the world.

This holistic approach to supply chain resilience makes this book unique. At the end of each chapter, professors will find a dedicated part, which will assist them in managing their in-class interaction with students. This book can be used as an academic compendium or as a guide for supply chain professionals who want to cement the resilience of their supply chains and successfully navigate through crisis.

Contents

Testimonials

"Supply Chain Resilience: Survival Strategies for Turbulent Times *is an insightful and practical guide to tackling the challenges of today's complex global supply chains. Andreas Karaoulanis blends clear explanations with real-world strategies, making it an essential resource for both professionals and students. This book doesn't just highlight the importance of resilience—it shows you how to achieve it, offering a valuable toolkit for building more sustainable and robust supply chains."*—**Dr. MALLON Steve (Director of research, Swiss School of Business Research)**

"This book is highly recommended for supply chain professionals and students alike. It provides a concise yet structured discussion on the crucial topic of supply chain resilience in today's fast-changing world, especially in the face of recent global disruptions. The author shares his extensive experience and knowledge in the field of supply chain management, making this book a practical guide for those looking to fortify their supply chains against unforeseen challenges."—**Dr. Lo Alex (Professor in Business and Sustainability, York St. John University)**

Preface

My name is Andreas Karaoulanis, and I am the author of this book. I started my academic journey about 10 years ago when I decided to leave the industry and try to transmit 25+ years of experience to new professionals and students. I saw that as an opportunity to change the world in the eyes of young people and believe that this was one of the most important changes/decisions in my life.

I have a diverse educational background which includes studies in engineering and business. My studies include a bachelor's and a master's degree in engineering from Greece, a master's and a MBA from Sweden, a DBA from Poland, while i am about to complete my PhD in business in a UK university.

I have been working in academia with universities, colleges and business schools from several countries, like UAE, Greece, Lithuania, Switzerland, The Netherlands, Italy.

Currently i am teaching business topics and conducting research with Kaunas Higher Education Institution Lithuania, supervising PhD students with SSBR Switzerland, teaching supply chain management at a master's level with Luis business school Amsterdam, teaching human resources management with Vytautas Magnus university Lithuania and teaching several business topics with Kronenburgh International business school the Netherlands.I have been teaching, till today, many business- and management-related topics, although in recent years, I have mainly focused on teaching supply chain-related ones.

I also am a researcher with a few dozen published papers, a peer reviewer in some major journals, and of course, an international author with (including this one) six published books with European and U.S. publishing houses.

I was not always an academic, as I have a long history in several industries like financing, retailing, apparel and fashion, automotive, publishing, manufacturing, and so on. As a professional, I had many experiences in different supply chains, and most importantly, during turbulent times, as I was working in supply chain-related positions in different industries in Greece during the big financial crisis that hit the country in 2010 and, of course, during the harsh years of the COVID-19 pandemic. Such experiences made me try to find ways to improve the resilience of the supply chains of the companies I was working with as they were struggling against phenomena that everybody in the market was encountering for the first time.

The recent COVID-19 pandemic that hit hard the whole of humanity and my home country's big financial crisis reminded me of something that most professionals sometimes tend to forget, that nothing can be taken for granted. Especially nowadays, in our globalized world, in which disruptions in, for example, Asia can have ripple effects in Europe or Australia and so on.

Supply chains during COVID-19 were a crucial element that affected the lives of millions. This was something that intrigued me so much, and when combined with my new position as a lecturer in supply chain management studies at both undergraduate and postgraduate levels, an inner urge motivated me to write this book.

The main purpose behind writing this book was twofold. First, I wanted to assist supply chain professionals and inspire them by providing, in the form of a concise handbook, information that sometimes due to the complexity and magnitude of their workload they tend to forget. Resilient supply chains are the future, and the recent unforeseen events of the COVID-19 pandemic, the Suez Canal blockage, the war in Ukraine, and the war in Gaza have already come to remind us how fragile our supply chains can be and that we need to do the best we can to fortify them as supply chain professionals.

The second purpose behind writing this book is to try to give, in a concise and dense form, information to supply chain students that can assist them towards a deeper understanding of the discipline.

The book is written in a very simple form. It is divided into two parts. The first one is subdivided into two chapters. The first chapter discusses supply chains in general, while the second chapter discusses the factors that can test the resilience of a given supply chain. In the second part, I present several important and well-tested strategies that supply chain professionals might choose to use and/or combine to enhance their supply chain resilience. The book concludes with the epilogue and the references table. I believe that this simple formation makes it very easy to read and comprehend, which was one of my major goals when I started writing.

Finally, I want to thank God, as without his grace I couldn't fulfill this mission. I also want to thank all my beloved family members for being my continuous inspiration and motivation during this journey.

The writing of this book wouldn't have been possible without the collaboration and trust of Business Expert Press with which I have already written two more books on business-related topics as well.

Making this world a better place should be everybody's number one priority. Creating resilient supply chains can be a big step toward that direction, as not only dissemination of goods, medicines, and so on can be safer, but also ethical collaborations can build long-lasting quality relationships between people and nations. Sustainability goes hand in hand with resilience. We need to try to not forget that and target more resilient and sustainable supply chains that will be the cornerstone for a better world to leave to our children.

Introduction

"The linkage of supply-related activities across multiple functions and organizations." This is how Banbury (1975, cited in Nakano, 2020) describes supply chains. From the above definition, it is obvious that supply chains can be seen as the link between not only multiple functions (e.g., procurement, purchasing, transportation, warehousing, etc.) but also between multiple organizations. This is extremely important because it can help us understand the multidimensional role that supply chains have in today's global markets. In addition, supply chains encompass activities that not only have to do with the transportation of goods from the source to the end user but also with their transformation from raw materials into goods (Hines, 2013). Supply chains are "service systems delivering value to consumers and customers; and contributing value to suppliers, producers and distributors" (Hines, 2013, p. 6).

Just after the COVID-19 pandemic and in the middle of the Ukraine–Russia war, the world is starting to realize not only the importance of the eurythmic operations of supply chains but also how fragile and interconnected they are on a global scale. The multidimensional role of supply chains for the global community is highlighted now, maybe more than ever, as we probably are on the verge of witnessing challenges that will have to do with energy, food supplies, medicine supplies, and so on, functions that are critical for the survival of our civilization.

Supply chain disruptions of many kinds are emerging, especially in the last few years, making supply chain management a difficult and complicated task (Turkman and McCormak, 2009). Well-known examples are, of course, the problems that the COVID-19 pandemic brought into the global supply chains, the war in Ukraine, but also incidents like the blockage of the Suez Canal, the vast logistics problems for the United Kingdom that followed Brexit, and so on.

The ongoing energy crisis has made it imperative for businesses all over the globe to optimize their supply chains to lower costs and improve their efficiency. As extra help during this difficult period, new technologies have emerged, which can make supply chain management more efficient and might be able to mitigate risks and deal effectively with the increased demand.

In addition to the above, supply chains today need to not only become more efficient and cope with the contemporary disruptions but also to be able to increase the offered value both upstream and downstream. Supply chain relationships need to evolve and maybe change their profile and directions, while new economic models need to be implemented in a way that they will be able to successfully face the economic challenges that arose in the last years due to the adverse situations that our world is facing.

Sustainability issues need to be addressed as well, since climate change creates problems not only for the global society but also increases the occurrence of adverse weather phenomena, which have negative results on transportation and logistics in general.

The shift, in the last years, in the information equilibrium between buyers and customers via the use of the Internet of things (IoT) and big data has also shifted the way that relationships and decision-making taking place inside a supply chain design. Information sharing between the different parts/members of a supply chain is extremely crucial for the overall supply chain visibility,[1] agility,[2] collaboration, and performance (Baah et al., 2022), something that also underlines the importance of adopting strategies that will be able to address such topics with success.

Control of the end-to-end processes of a supply chain is essential nowadays to establish a seamless flow of goods on a global scale (Martin and Hollweg, 2021).

---

1   Supply chain visibility: "supply chain visibility is the ability of products or services to be analysed and tracked during their lifespan." (Inboundlogistics.com, 2023)
2   Supply chain agility: "Supply chain agility refers to a company's ability to quickly adjust its strategy, particularly in procurement, inventory management and delivery to meet rapidly changing supply chain requirements." (gep.com, n.d.)

PART I

The only constant is change —Heraclitus

CHAPTER 1

What Is Supply Chain Resilience

I n this chapter we are going to see some definitions of what do we mean by the term "supply chain resilience." A short discussion will follow in terms of some general characteristics that will be addressed.

Supply Chain Resilience—Definition

Supply chain resilience, especially in the last few years, has became a very hot topic. Companies realized that they need to improve it to strengthen their competitive advantage and sustain their business. But what do we mean by the term "supply chain resilience"? There are several definitions that address the topic. In the following lines, we are going to stress some of the most insightful and straightforward ones.

According to the Cambridge Dictionary, resilience is "the quality of being able to return quickly to a previous good condition after problems" (Dictionary.cambridge.org, n.d.). As we can understand from that definition, supply chain resilience is an important quality of supply chains that companies need to develop and maintain in order to be able to base their survival on their resilient supply chain if and/or when, for example, a natural or an unnatural disaster might occur.

According to Hohenstein et al. (2015), supply chain resilience is "the ability to be prepared for unexpected risk events, responding and recovering quickly to potential disruptions." So, according to this definition, we see that another element is added to the Cambridge Dictionary's definition that we discussed in the previous paragraph, the "being prepared for unexpected risk events." So, we can say that to try to define supply chain resilience, we need to take into consideration the capability to act proactively in a way to be able to mitigate potential unforeseen threats in our supply chain.

According to another interesting definition, supply chain resilience can be defined as "the property of supply chains to handle impending vulnerabilities and potential disruptions" (Rajesh, 2017). This definition sounds more generic and tends to deal with the capability of a supply chain to deal with disruptions that are about to happen. In other words, this definition tends to take a more "last minute" capability of supply chains to deal with disruptions. Of course, it is obvious from this definition that since the disruption is about to happen, some kind of forecasting mechanism should be in place, or some kind of precautionary approach should exist, in terms of how to deal with potential threats that might affect negatively the supply chain, but this is not very clear.

According to a definition by Yazdanparast et al. (2021, 2018), supply chain resilience can be seen "as an effective strategic planning during disturbances, which is a way to mitigate supply chain vulnerabilities." From that definition we can see that supply chain resilience is the part of the strategic planning that deals with supply chain vulnerabilities. This definition is very useful because it helps us incorporate the strategic component in our supply chain definition. So, according to Yazdanparast's et al. (2021, 2018) definition, we can only see supply chain resilience as part of our overall supply chain strategy on a company level.

According to a newsletter from Harvard Business School Publishing and the MIT Center for Transportation and Logistics, titled "Building a Resilient Supply Chain" (Yossi, 2005), supply chain resilience "no longer implies merely the ability to manage risk. It now assumes that the ability to manage risks means being better positioned than competitors to deal with and even gain advantage from disruptions." This definition introduces in our discussion the element of competitive advantage through positioning against competitors. This element is also crucial as it reminds us that supply chain resilience can be used as a powerful weapon in terms of building our competitive advantage, especially during a period of crisis.

Another interesting definition of supply chain resilience comes from Fiksel (2006), from his paper titled "Sustainability and Resilience: Toward a Systems Approach." According to Fiksel (2006), supply chain resilience is the capacity that a system must have to survive, adapt, and grow in the face of turbulent change.

What we see from all the above-mentioned definitions of supply chain resilience is that they involve many elements that all have to do with the same goal, to efficiently deal with disruptions/risks that might appear in a supply chain. Table 1.1 is giving us an overview of all the definitions that we discussed till now.

As we can see from Table 1.1, supply chain resilience involves many elements that position it as a strategic component, an important part of the strategic planning process that helps to mitigate disruptions that are about to occur in the future. The term also describes the capability and quality of the supply chain in terms of dealing with such

Table 1.1 Examined definitions of supply chain resilience

Source	Definition
Cambridge Dictionary	"The quality of being able to return quickly to a previous good condition after problems"
Hohenstein et al. (2015)	"The ability to be prepared for unexpected risk events, responding and recovering quickly to potential disruptions, is presented"
Rajesh (2017)	"The property of supply chains to handle impending vulnerabilities and potential disruptions"
Yazdanparast et al. (2021, 2018)	"As an effective strategic planning during disturbances, which is a way to mitigate supply chain vulnerabilities"
Yossi (2005)	"No longer implies merely the ability to manage risk. It now assumes that the ability to manage risks, means being better positioned than competitors to deal with and even gain advantage from disruptions"
Fiksel (2006)	"The capacity of a system to survive, adapt and grow in the face of turbulent change"

disruptions, especially in a way that, via the right positioning, it can create a competitive advantage for the company in question.

In the following subchapter, the importance of supply chain resilience will be highlighted.

Importance of Supply Chain Resilience

Supply chains, on a global level, faced and still face a lot of challenges which makes them less functional, something which makes even more dramatic the absence of resilience. Global events like the incident in the Suez Canal, the COVID-19 pandemic, or the war in Ukraine, and so on have imposed huge pressure on global supply chains, something which highlights the importance of their resilience. In the following Figure 1.1, we can see the fluctuations of the Global Supply Chain Pressure Index (GSCPI)[*] in a period of 24 years (from 1998 till 2022).

GSCPI is an extremely important index that can be used to provide a comprehensive summary of potential supply chain disruptions (newyorkfed.org. n.d.), It can be used in order to help us understand in a more comprehensive way the impact of global supply chain pressures. Also, it can be used in order to help us gauge the importance of

1998–2022

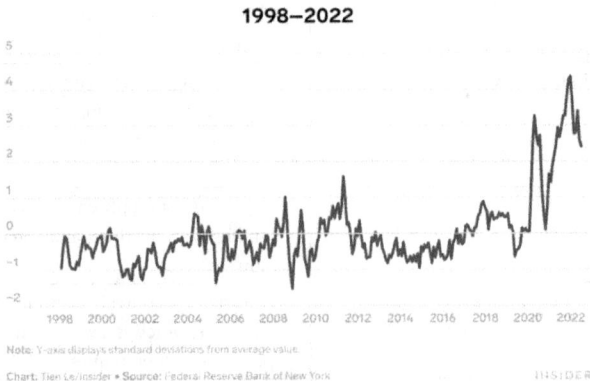

Figure 1.1 Global supply chain pressure index (Safane 2022)

[*] Global Supply Chain Pressure Index: The Global Supply Chain Pressure Index (GSCPI) is a new measurement of supply chain conditions, created by the Federal Reserve Bank of New York. The index combines variables from several indices in transportation and manufacturing, such as those related to delivery times, prices, and inventory (Safane 2022).

global supply chain constraints as they can create ripple effects taht can significantly damage supply chains (newyorkfed. org) that might create ripple effects and cause significant damage to our supply chain. In other words, via this index, which is updated at or shortly after 10:00 a.m. on the fourth business day of each month (newyorkfed.org. n.d.), we can be informed about the global supply chain pressures on time, something that can help toward taking measures that can improve our supply chain's resilience.

Since the Y (Vertical) axis in GSCPI calculates the standard deviation from the average value and the X (Horizontal) axis represents the years that we study, we can easily see that there is a huge deviation from the average during the COVID-19 pandemic, something which means that the global supply chains were facing major disruptions during that period. In the following figure (Figure 1.2), we can see that in the beginning of the COVID-19 pandemic, we started having the first signals that some disruption is hitting the global supply chains. This was a warning signal for supply chain professionals to start taking measures to enhance their supply chain robustness and/or resilience, although such measures need to be proactive and not to solve the problem when it is here (Figure 1.2).

According to Alfarsi et al. (2019), in recent years, most companies have become even more vulnerable to disruptions exactly because of their supply chains which, due to the global economy, have become longer (since now they include more tiers), larger (since they have more

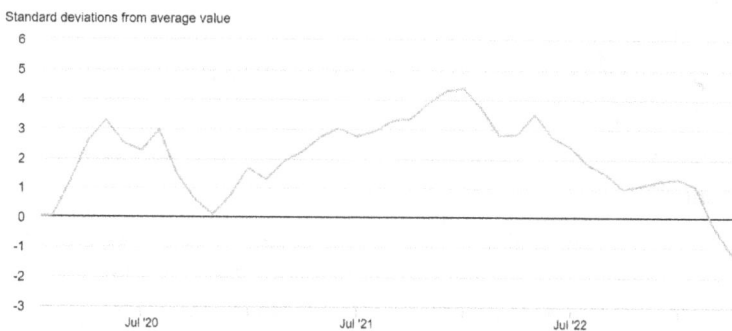

Figure 1.2 Global supply chain pressure index during the COVID-19 pandemic (newyorkfed.org. n.d.)

depth), and of course, they have become more complex in total. This is why Waters (2011) underlines that the longer the supply chain, the less reliable it is. So we can understand that since supply chains today are usually longer and more complex, mainly due to their international nature, inevitably they have an increased vulnerability.

A vulnerable supply chain can create a lot of problems in so many ways for our business. This is why mechanisms like the ones that improve resilience need to be built.

Another point of consideration might also be that according to Alfarsi et al. (2019), firm reputation is an element of business that can heavily be impacted in a negative way by a decreased supply chain resilience. This has to do with the supply chain's responsiveness which can be negatively affected by a disrupted link of logistics operations. Both upstream and downstream operations can hurt the reliability of the supply chain, as disruptions might occur not only in terms of transportation of goods and raw materials, but also in terms of manufacturing as we will see in Chapter 2. Such elements of supply chain are also extremely crucial in terms of building its resilience and since resilience can harm business reputation is obvious that supply chain resilience can be the critical factor that might decide the survival of the business, especially during turbulent times.

Also Wong et al. (2020) underlines that according to empirical evidence, supply chain resilience was found to be positively related to several, crucial for business, factors, like risk management, market, and financial performance. Especially its contribution to risk management and market performance, when firms experience catastrophic disruptions, for example, in their infrastructure, can be a catalyst for the firm's recovery.

Moreover, risk management can be a decisive factor that can drastically increase supply chain resilience. The identification of potential risks in our supply chain and their mitigation via the use of risk management mechanisms can not only increase supply chain robustness but it can also enhance its resilience, as the less risks involved the less are the threats to our supply chain and the better and quicker is its recovery, In addition, scenario planning (especially nowadays via the use of artificial intelligence) can be a decisive paragon that can help us increase supply chain resilience as we are going to be better prepared for different scenarios that might occur in the near future.

Risk management plays a significant role in increasing supply chain resilience as the identified potential risks can assist companies to develop contingency plans and get prepared for unexpected disasters. Because of that, companies can achieve continuity of their operations and meet their customers' demand, while they can reduce their costs by identifying areas of waste and/or inefficiency (e.g., by optimizing inventory levels, reduce carrying costs, reduce risk of stockouts, and so on.) (McGrath and Jonker 2023)

In addition to risk management, market and financial performance can also enhance supply chain resilience, as a financially stable and robust company can invest in innovations, new technologies, better infrastructure, can become more flexible (e.g., via supplier base differentiation or even strong relationships with suppliers (e.g., Japanese Keiretsus), increased security buffers, and so on) and therefore more resilient.

Moreover, strong market performance can be a catalyst toward supply chain resilience, as companies can leverage insights from market research to predict potential disruptions that might hit their supply chains., Therefore they can take precautionary measures when needed, or in a proactive way, in order to rebound quicker during crisis.

An interesting point here is that when companies try to evaluate the level of investment that is required in order to enhance their supply chain resilience, they need to know how much they need to increase their supply chain resilience, something which is very difficult to say as there is no precise measure and/or mechanism to gauge supply chain resilience (Rice et al. 2022). Therefore, they can only estimate the associated investment, something which makes very difficult to allocate a specific amount that might be needed for such an important investment (Rice et al. 2022).

On the same wavelength, Stephens et al. (2022) highlight that supply chain resilience is strongly connected to market performance. They also add that supply chain disruption orientation, which can lead the company in question to the implementation of a supply chain resilience framework on a proactive basis, is also critical and a prerequisite. In that way the company in question would be able to cultivate a resiliency character which will help it to recover when this kind of disruption appears (Stephens et al. 2022).

High market uncertainty also can be positively mitigated by the implementation of a supply chain resilience framework (Aslam et al. 2020). In addition, supply chain ambidexterity can be seen as a very important paragon, which can mitigate market uncertainty, but which can also, as we will see in Chapter 3, increase resilience in our supply chain (Aslam et al. 2020). This is in line with the Wong et al.'s (2020) research which we briefly discussed a few paragraphs previously.

Gu et al. (2020, 2021) also underline the role of ambidexterity when they break down in their research, the positive impact of supply chain resilience to the whole supply chain operations performance. They highlight that both supplier and customer resilience could improve supply chain performance (Gu et al., 2020, 2021).

The reconfiguration of the supply chain in the face of future disruptions is one of the most important positive influences that supply chain resilience can have in the overall performance of the company (Al Naimi et al. 2021) and can be achieved easier via a culture of agility, collaboration, and risk management (Al Naimi et al. 2021). Especially when pursuing supply chain integration and supply chain reconfiguration simultaneously as part of an ambidextrous supply chain management,[†] is the key in terms of helping manufacturers to gain superior performance (Lee and Neil 2021). This is supported by the research of Lee and Neil (2021) on 333 Taiwanese manufacturing firms which demonstrated that ambidextrous management of supply chains can have a positive effect on manufacturer performance. Since increased manufacturing performance can increase profits, more investments can take place on infrastructure, new technologies, and so on, as we have

---

[†] Ambidextrous supply chain: "Organizational ambidexterity is the simultaneous act of exploiting existing competences and exploring new opportunities" (Partanen et al. 2020).

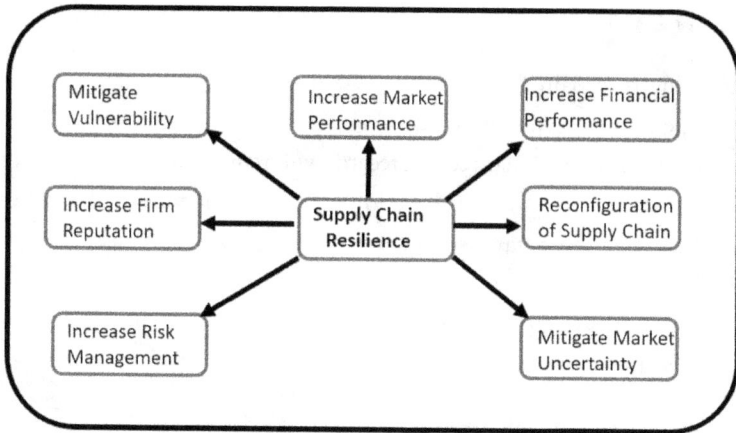

Figure 1.3 Business paragons that are influenced by increased supply chain resilience

already discussed, something that can enhance supply chain resilience (Lee and Neil, 2021).

As we can see from the above, the importance of supply chain resilience for business is huge, as it is heavily involved in many ways in so many important business elements like performance improvement, mitigation of market uncertainty, increase market performance, and so on, which can lead to increased financial performance and increased firm reputation via the increased responsiveness that it can bring, reduced vulnerability in terms of potential disruptions, and so on. In Figure 1.3, we can see the paragons that highlight the importance of supply chain resilience.

Is Resilience the Future of Supply Chains?

As we discussed till now, supply chain resilience is a very important paragon that impacts supply chain operations. But what about the near future? Is supply chain resilience something on which companies need to focus? Should they base their supply chain operations on their resilience plans? In the following paragraphs, we will look at how big multinationals in the consulting and logistics industry are approaching the topic.

Bain & Co

According to a Bain & Co report (Weforum.org 2022), "Supply chain and operations teams must develop new capabilities—and quickly. Playing to a more balanced scorecard will require a lot of changes: reducing the carbon footprint, building greater resilience in the supply chain, creating more transparency, and ensuring accountability,"

This statement per se is indicative of the continuously increasing importance of supply chain resilience for that organization, especially in the years after the COVID-19 pandemic.

Deloitte

According to Deloitte (n.d.), supply chains are at the epicenter of the planning of both government and public services organizations, as they are striving to deliver value to the public in the most possibly effective and efficient way. This is crucial, especially when it comes to resilience during disruption times as it is when mission-ready organizations strive to ensure that operations and supply chain management practices are set up to success (Deloitte n.d.). Therefore, Deloitte understands the importance of supply chain resilience, especially turbulent times.

Maersk

Maersk (2021) underlines that the last pandemic and its aftermath was a very good lesson for supply chain professionals all over the world. According to a survey that was conducted by the Business Continuity Institute (Maersk 2021), between 526 respondents across 64 countries, 34 percent reported a decrease in their annual earnings of €1 million or above, which was caused by supply chain disruptions (Maersk 2021). This fact per se is extremely important and highlights how crucially important it is for companies to enhance their supply chain resilience, especially since disruptions that might occur in one part of the world can negatively influence almost everybody on the planet.

PwC

PwC.nl (2022), indicates, in the same wavelength, that resilience is a very important factor that will vastly affect supply chains in the near future. More specifically, disruptions are now taking place on a global scale and increasingly pushing companies toward the resilience of their supply chains (PwC.nl 2022). Such global disruptions increase unpredictability, thus risks, something that makes more important for companies to be able to move quickly in their supply chains to be able to maintain both production and distribution in the best possible way (PwC.nl 2022).

Kuehne–Nagel

As one of the biggest four PLs in the world, Kuehne–Nagel understands that the last pandemic exposed several systemic flaws in the companies' supply chain operations, especially since modern supply chains were constructed in a way that they can reach an equilibrium between high standards of performance and as low as possible costs (Kuehne–Nagel n.d.). As a result, long, extended and highly complex systems were implemented, something that lowered visibility and, on many occasions, lacked the placement of critical safeguards against potential disruptions (Kuehne–Nagel n.d.).

Kuehne–Nagel (n.d.) reaches to the conclusion that all of this has demonstrated the need for increased resilience in global supply chains and highlighted the need for supply chain managers to start learning to live with and manage disruption on an ongoing basis. As they say "Just-in-case appears to be replacing just-in-time as the order of the day" (Kuehne–Nagel n.d.). It is inevitable that there is a global shift that is taking place in the last years and that will continue to take place in the years to come. This is a shift from maximum efficiency at the lower cost toward the goal of ensuring a robust and resilient supply chain (Kuehne–Nagel n.d.).

Components of Supply Chain Resilience

Information Flow

Supply chain resilience is the result of serious teamwork. To achieve it, supply chain professionals need to adopt a holistic view of their supply chain. Professional silos always have negative results, as information flow needs to be unbiased and without restrictions or miscontinuations. A good level of information/communication which will be able to improve visibility and downsize the time of response to unpredicted disruptions can be achieved by inclusivity. Inclusivity, which might take place for example, via a 360° feedback, can be seen as a critical supply chain resilience element as it is a decisive paragon in terms of successful decision making which can enhance supply chain resilience.

Factors that can facilitate both inclusivity and good communication/information flow across a supply chain are good management, good organization structure which eliminates work silos and cluttered communication, both horizontally and vertically, and of course, an open and inclusive company culture which can foster a high teamwork spirit.

Upstream Communication[‡] and Collaboration

Another very important component of supply chain resilience is the upstream relationships of the company in question, namely, the ones with the first, second, or third tier suppliers. This is crucial since it can help the supply chain in question to strengthen its response during disruptions and unforeseen negative incidents. A strong supplier network can ensure disturbance avoidance in the supply of raw materials during disruptions and the downsizing of the supplier risk (e.g., in case we have many suppliers). Decisions on the supplier base can be facilitated via tools like the Kraljic Matrix[§] and so on.

[‡] Upstream supply chain: "The upstream supply chain includes all activities related to the organization's suppliers: those parties that source raw material inputs to send to the manufacturer" (Britt 2021).

[§] Kraljic Matrix: "A key part of supply chain management is segmenting the vendor base. From there, organizations can match design supplier relationship management strategies against this map of suppliers. The Kraljic Matrix is one

In addition, international companies need to understand their position in the global supply chain and how local disruptions might affect their operations, like transportation, warehousing, distribution, and so on. Solutions like the Japanese Keiretsus, which will be discussed in Chapter 3, are good examples on how companies can leverage a good relationship with their suppliers. The question here is "what if the company in question has an international character? How feasible are solutions like that?"

Downstream[¶] Communication and Relationships

As we have already discussed, good communication and information flow is crucial for our supply chain resilience. As we also discussed, good communication not only involves communication that takes place inside the company and has to do with vertical and horizontal communication but also involves communication with suppliers. In addition, downstream communication, which is the company's communication with its customers, is also crucial as it can help the company in question to mitigate problems like the bullwhip effect, which can create dangerous disruptions that can spread quickly along the whole supply chain and which we will also discuss in Chapter 3.

Communication with the end customer can take many forms and can be achieved in many ways. One way is by receiving the information, on a retail level, by catching new demand and/or fluctuations in demand. Another way is to be able to reach the heartbeat of the market by asking customers and understand their needs and trends in their buying behavior. Business, thus, supply chain professionals need to always have an eye in the market to be able not only to have a thorough understanding of their competitors and their customers but also to be always ready to smell in the air potential threats or disruption that might occur. This "sense" of the market is crucial as it will put them

_____

of the most effective ways to deliver accurate supplier segmentation" (Webb 2017).

¶ Downstream supply chain: The downstream supply chain refers to activities postmanufacturing, namely distributing the product to the final customer (Britt 2021).

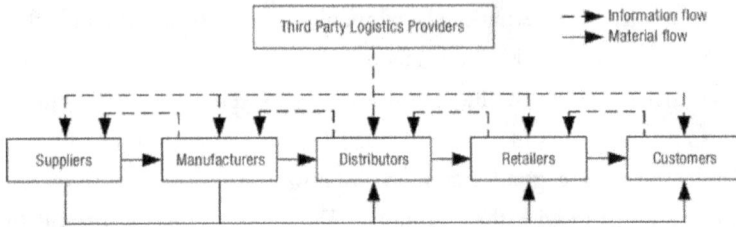

Figure 1.4 Supply chain flows (adapted from Min and Zhou 2002)
(Pinho et al. 2015)

one move ahead of their competitors and it can provide them with a time advantage in an upcoming crisis.

In addition to the above, good relationships with the customers can create a climate of trust and collaboration which can guarantee a win–win situation between both parties as they can support each other during disruptions. This support can have for example, the form of payments via installments for the customers, something which can assist them in terms of continuing ordering during disrupted times, while the seller company can feel safe enough in terms of receiving its money. In that way, supply chains can be more operational during crisis, something which is a sign of an enhanced supply chain resilience.

What is also important is not to break the communication chain, because that will disturb the information flow along the supply chain. The communication/information flow/chain is depicted in Figure 1.4.

As we can see in the above figure, information thus communication takes place along the supply chain and involves all its nodes (from suppliers till the end customer and third-party logistics providers (3PLs), and so on).

Supply Chain Visibility

It is very important for our supply chain to have very good end-to-end visibility. If such visibility can be achieved, it means that information flow is good and that we are able to know exactly what is going on, in terms of, for example, potential disruptions, throughout our supply chain. In that way our supply chain robustness will be dramatically increased, something which will create ripple effects that will positively affect our supply chain's resilience too. So, this leads us to another very important component of supply chain resilience which is good visibility both upstream and downstream.

Since visibility and communication are two crucial supply chain resilience components, it is important to facilitate them in the best possible way. This facilitation can also be achieved via the use of new technologies. Of course it can also be achieved via team spirit and enhanced collaboration, thus communication.

So it can be said that if we want to implement a resilient supply chain, we need to create an end-to-end visible one. This visibility can help us because it can become the springboard for decision making, which now can be based on a more holistic basis, thus it can be more accurate and towards the right direction.

To increase this visibility, we need the assistance of technology (GEP.com 2021). Automation and digitization can improve node-to-node and end-to-end supply chain visibility in an efficient and holistic way. Supply chain control towers,[**] Electronic Data Interchange (EDI), software like WMS (Warehouse Management Systems), ERP (Enterprise Resource Planning), use of IoT technologies, and so on, are only some of the systems/technologies that we can use in order to increase visibility, thus communication and information flow along our supply chain.

Supply Chain Agility

Agility is another important component of supply chain resilience, as it has to do with adapting, especially during times of crisis, and finding new ways to create value, thus managing change effectively (GEP.com 2021).

According to Tarafdar et al. (2017), supply chain agility corresponds to an increase in supply chain performance as well, something which can be also seen as a factor that can positively contribute to an increased

---

[**] Supply chain control towers: "A supply chain control tower is a centralized platform that provides real-time data and analytics to help companies manage their supply chains. It gives managers a complete view of the supply chain and makes informed decisions that can improve efficiency and optimize costs" (edureka.co. 2022).

Table 1.2 Components of a resilient supply chain

Components of a Resilient Supply Chain
Holistic view/no silos
Inclusivity
Visibility
Communication/information flow
Management/decision making
Use of new technologies
Agility

supply chain resilience. This is a logical connection especially since supply chain agility and resilience are very closely related. To increase the resilience of a given supply chain via its increased agility, communication is again the key. That communication, apart from internal, needs to also be external, in terms of building relationships with both suppliers and customers, as according to Power et al. (2001), agility increases the more customer-focused we are.

In Table 1.2, we can see the main components of a resilient supply chain.

Resilience Metrics/Indexes

Supply chain resilience is very important for any given company, especially nowadays as we experience an international environment, which maybe more than ever in recent years, can become turbulent, volatile, and difficult—if not impossible—to predict at any time. This is the reason why it becomes more important to be able to gauge the degree of resilience that our supply chain has achieved. Toward that direction, several supply chain metrics have been introduced in the last years. In this subchapter, we are going to present the most important of them.

TTR: *Time to Recovery*

The first metric that attempts to quantify supply chain resilience is the Time To Recovery (TTR) metric. According to several scholars

(Simchi et al. 2014; Sodhi and Tang 2009, cited in Golnar et al. 2020), this can be considered as an appropriate quantitative resilience metric. The quantification of supply chain resilience via this metric, comes by measuring the time that is needed for the supply chain in question to return to its normal operations after the disruption (Golnar et al. 2020).

So, TTR can be defined as the time needed for a specific node (like a supplier facility, a distribution center (DC), or a transportation hub, and so on.), to be restored to its full functionality after a disruption (Simchi-Levi et al. 2014).

TTR can be calculated by examining historical data and by getting answers from the company's buyers and suppliers (via e.g., the use of a questionnaire, and so on). In that way, we can get the TTR values which can be either unique for every node in our supply chain, or they can differ across a subset of different nodes (Simchi-Levi et al. 2014).

RLO: *Recovery Level Objective*

This is another important supply chain resilience metric. It is important because it can assist us in determining important information for our supply chain recovery after a serious disruption (Kirvan 2022). This important information usually includes data files and databases that we want to recover, applications that are crucial to restart, network resources that need to return to service in the before-the-crisis state, critical business processes that also need to be restored, the rejoining with employees who need to be in a mental and physical condition to start working again, and so on (Kirvan 2022).

LPR: *Lost Performance During Recovery*

This metric is also very important as it can provide us with valuable information regarding the deviation of our supply chain's performance after the disruption took place from our supply chain's baseline performance.

What is important here is to underline that the difference between the previous two performances can be considered only during the recovery period (Behzadi et al. 2020). Also, we need to keep in mind, that this metric mostly gauges cost/profit—or quality during the recovery interval that we are facing (Hishamuddin et al. 2013; Saghafian and Van Oyen 2016; Zobel 2011, cited in Behzadi et al. 2020).

TTS: Time to Survive

Survival in supply chains can take several forms. One of the most important is being able to reach certain levels of production and/or distribution so that demand will be matched. If demand will be matched, then we can say that survival, at least at a certain level, can be reached. So here is when we need to use the so-called TTS metric. This metric indicates whether, during the disruption period in a specific facility, a company continues to be able to keep matching demand (Guillot 2018).

The TTS calculation is important as it can assist an organization to manage its supply chain in terms of challenges and opportunities that might appear (Guillot 2018). By recording their TTS, organizations can depict their entire supply chain with, for example, a flow chart that will start from upstream and end at the downstream facilities. In that way, it will be able to pinpoint what is needed in each DC to match demand (Guillot 2018).

There are other supply chain metrics, like the Net Present Value of Lost Profit (NPV-LP), efficiency of recovering to normality, performance of discerning possible disruptions, damage from disruptions, and so on (Yuhan et al. 2020). What we always need to have in mind is that there are some other parameters that we need to take into consideration, which are not easily quantifiable, like collaboration (internal and external), inclusiveness, leadership, and so on.

Gauging the resilience of our supply chain is a very important task as it will give us an understanding of what "is going on" in our supply chain this very instance and what might have been the damages that were provoked by the disruption in question. This knowledge is extremely valuable in terms of helping us understand what we should do to successfully face potential problems that were caused by a disruption in our supply chain.

Although the use of supply chain resilience-related metrics can be crucial, supply chain professionals are the ones who need to understand the situation and use in a productive way all the info provided by the analysis of the data that came from their metrics. In other words, supply chain professionals need to have both the knowledge and the experience to interpret the given metrics in the right way to make the right decisions and make the right movements that will enhance the overall supply chain resilience and strengthen their supply chain.

Examples of Companies That Have Developed a Resilient Supply Chain

Although developing a resilient supply chain is not a very easy thing to do, it is imperative that companies effectively deal with it. Especially multinational companies with very complex supply chains need to understand that implementing resilience strategies in their supply chains is one paragon that can increase their survival chances when disruption occurs. In a very competitive global environment, being resilient in terms of one's supply chain can be the decisive factor that can lead the company in question in acquiring the competitive advantage that it needs in order not only to survive but also to thrive.

Several well-known companies have managed to strengthen their supply chain resilience via their dedicated strategies. A few examples of such companies are the following.

Walmart

Walmart is a well-known U.S.-based company with more than 5,300 stores in the country and other 5,200 stores worldwide, while the company employs more than 2.1 million people (Statista, cited in Just Imagination Blog 2022). The company has a quite complex supply chain which for example, includes around 210 DCs (Just Imagination Blog 2022). It is easy to understand that the company's shipping fleet drives hundreds of millions of miles every year (Just Imagination Blog 2022). When the COVID-19 pandemic crisis hit the globe, Walmart dealt with the problems that were induced in its supply chains by chartering its own ships to unload to less-busy ports, while the company plans to open new fulfillment centers, which will be using more automation technology that will allow much faster order processing, something that will help the company to reduce dramatically its lead times (Just Imagination Blog 2022). In that way, Walmart managed not only to survive during crisis but also to become very competitive and to enhance both its supply chain robustness and resilience.

Of course, the cost that is involved in such a strategy is quite high. Therefore, companies like Walmart need to consider delivering a cost–benefit analysis before implementing such strategies in order to make sure that the increased costs are worth the investment as the benefits will be high as well.

3M

3M is a big U.S. company that took the initiative from previous pandemics like SARS and therefore was well prepared to deal with, for example, the COVID-19 supply chain crisis. As of 2020, the company took the initiative and implemented an operational change to help itself to cope with the increase in production needed to addressing a potential surge in demand that might occur, for example, due to a pandemic (Just Imagination Blog 2022).

The company was the producer of the N95 masks during the COVID-19 pandemic. Since the company was prepared for such situations, when the COVID-19 pandemic broke out, it was able and ready to immediately maximize its production to meet demand. But although in that way, the company became more robust against such disruptions, it was still possible for other problems that had to do with resilience to take place (e.g., fluctuations in production and demand, stocks needed, and so on). Toward that direction, since the height of the pandemic, the company implemented a system of tracking down production levels to make sure that they are sufficient and capable of following the current demand patterns (Just Imagination Blog 2022). Such strategic steps led to an increased supply chain resilience which made the company able to successfully navigate through the dark waters of the COVID-19 pandemic.

Small Business' Supply Chain Resilience

Small and Medium Enterprises (SMEs) are the backbone of society. Therefore, it is extremely important to survive during crisis, as the opposite will have devastating results for the societies in which they operate.

Under this prism, it is important to understand how such small companies can enhance their supply chain resilience and mitigate quickly the outcomes of a potential disaster.

One element that can assist SMEs to increase their supply chain resilience is collaboration. An important element that characterizes the way SMEs collaborate in a supply chain context, is relationships. Relational aspects of their partnerships need to combine contractual and relational investments thar depend on the business model, the business philosophy of the CEO of the small business, and the allocation of power within the supply chain (Trunk and Birkel 2022).

Especially when collaborations take place between the small business and their suppliers, contractual investments are higher (Trunk and Birkel 2022). Therefore we can understand that when we refer to small business and their partnerships in their respective supply chains, focus should be put on building relationships to create resilience in the supply chain (Trunk and Birkel 2022).

We need to understand that small business usually struggle with several challenges which might include financing difficulties, tight deadlines in terms of goods' deliveries and contracts to follow, supply chain bottlenecks, supply chain disruptions of all kinds, and of course, stiff competition in a globalized world (supplychaingamechanger.com 2024)

It is obvious from the above, that SMEs in order to be able to deal with such problems and increase the resilience of their supply chains need to develop certain mechanisms that will assist them toward that direction. Such mechanisms might be, for example, the implementation of a contingency plan (supplychaingamechanger.com 2024). Such a plan can be of low cost and can include emergency

response protocols, pinpointing alternative suppliers, and start prelimi-
nary discussions for potential future collaboration, establishing clear
communication channels that will be used during the crisis (supply-
chaingamechanger.com 2024). Of course, such a plan needs periodically
to be checked and to be updated (supplychaingamechanger.com 2024).

Another problematic area in terms of how SMEs are operating and
can negatively affect their supply chain resilience is the area of inventory
handling. According to recent research, 43 percent of SMEs in the
United States do not track their inventory! This is almost half of the
SMEs that operate in the United States. This is a big problem for
SMEs because, for example, during a crisis, they might not be able to
rebound because they might have their capital blocked in their excessive
inventory (supplychaingamechanger.com 2024). The solution to that
problem which can also enhance SMEs' supply chain resilience might
be the adaption of a lean inventory management approach which will
be based on demand–forecasting mechanisms and the setup of just-in-
time inventory systems that will assist them to maintain lean inventory
(supplychaingamechanger.com 2024). In that way, when crisis will arise,
they will be able to utilize all the capital they have and use it in a way
that will help them to increase their resilience and rebound from the
crisis to their previous state. Of course one thing that needs to be taken
under consideration from SME owners in terms of this strategy is the
cost of such forecasting mechanisms which will also be based on data
gathering and analyzing systems that need to be implemented.

Since supply chain resilience involves adaptation to new circumstances that crisis have brought upon SMEs and since SMEs usually do
not have enough capital to invest for example, in new cutting-edge
technologies, one thing that they can do to improve their supply chain
resilience is to both upskill[††] and reskill[‡‡] their employees (Mills et al.
2022).

Another important strategy that SMEs need to adapt to increase
their supply chain resilience is to strengthen their access to financing,

---

[††] Upskilling: "The process of learning new skills or of teaching workers new
skills" (dictionary.cambridge.org n.d.).
[‡‡] Reskilling: "The process of learning new skills so you can do a different job,
or of training people to do a different job" (dictionary.cambridge.org n.d.).

something that can be proved crucial, during crisis in helping them to recover and return to their previous status as quickly as possible (Mills et al. 2022). Since they will probably need to address several problems during the recovery period, one of which might be increased prices of products, disrupted supply chains which might need inventory buffers, lower demand which might hurt their liquidity, and so on. Facing such problems without access to capital might prove very difficult, something that might hurt the company's supply chain resilience.

Finally, another important element that SMEs need to have in mind is that if they want to improve their resilience, they need to be able to adapt an operations mindset/capability for fast changeovers[§§] and to use a wide range of products and shipment types (pnc.com 2024). The adaptation of fast changeovers will allow the company in question to adapt to changes when for example, one product might not have demand due to unforeseen circumstances that arrived during the crisis. For example, during the COVID-19 pandemic, due to lockdowns, many companies seized their production because nobody was buying their products and therefore, they needed to stop producing them in order to lower their production costs. Some of them were even ready to shift their production toward a different product that was in high demand, even during the lockdowns: masks. This made them thrive and not only did they present a resilient face of their supply chain but they also turned crisis into an opportunity for bigger profits.

In addition, the use of a wide range of products and shipments will make them more agile, something that will assist them to rebound quickly during crisis as, for example, their supply chain and/or distribution networks will not be fragmented as they will be able to use some of their alternative ones.

Notes for the Teacher

In this first chapter, we discussed supply chain resilience in a generic way. We gave its definition, and we highlighted specific elements like its importance and its components, while we gave some of the most

[§§] Fast changeover: "The ability to shift production from one unit or part to another very quickly" (pnc.com 2024).

important and most used supply chain resilience metrics. We also presented examples of some famous companies that managed to develop a resilient supply chain, while we discussed the future of supply chain resilience, and we made a short comment regarding the importance of relationships in terms of supply chain resilience in small business today.

Suggested Discussion Points

1. Why supply chain resilience is important for companies, especially nowadays?
2. CASES: Discussions about the companies presented: which are the characteristics of their supply chains that makes them resilient, what did they gain by having a resilient supply chain, why/if the resilience of their supply became/can become their competitive advantage in their industries
3. Discussion on the supply chain resilience metrics. How to be used in an already existent supply chain, if they can be used in a global supply chain, which might be potential challenges, why and how they can be important for the companies in question?
4. Discussion on any ideas which other metrics might be important for the resilience of a given supply chain and with which other operational metrics they might be combined.
5. Discussion on whether small business can implement a resilient supply chain. Is that doable from, for example, an economic perspective? Should they focus on their local distribution network or on the global one? Why a resilient supply chain is even more important for small businesses than it is for big corporations? Small business' supply chain resilience is affected by the resilience of the supply chains of bigger corporations. Is there something that small business can/need to do about that? Is it doable?, and so on.

CHAPTER 2

Critical Factors That Can Test a Supply Chain's Resilience

Resilience in the supply chain can be influenced by several factors like scarcity of raw materials, changes in international regulations, shortages in workforce, increase in logistics costs, occurrence of natural disasters, different kinds of unnatural incidents (e.g., the recent blockage of the Suez Canal etc.), shortages in critical manufacturing components (e.g., the recent shortage in chips etc.,) financing problems. In this chapter we are going to discuss those critical factors in terms of how they can test the existing supply chain resilience. Although such factors can test supply chains in terms of their resilience, they can be tackled by supply chains that are resilient, while others, less or no resilient at all, might not be able to deal with them and survive after a severe event e.g., natural disaster, and so on.

Scarcity of Raw Materials

According to Eskhenazi (2021), raw material prices are skyrocketing, not to mention that it is very difficult to find them in the first place. Warnings are coming from the *Financial Times*, Coca-Cola, Whirlpool, Procter & Gamble, Kimberly-Clark, and so on that prices of their final products are going to be increased to offset the rising costs of raw materials (Eskhenazy 2021).

When raw materials have to do with food, then things become even more critical, as now we can speak of a humanitarian crisis. Since the increase in food prices will inevitably lead many people to not be able to afford them. The Food and Agriculture Organization of the United Nations price index has reached its highest point in the last six years (Eskhenazi 2021). The World Bank denotes that this increase in global food prices inevitably leads to an epidemic of hunger throughout the world (Eskhenazi 2021).

Another dimension of the raw materials' scarcity (especially the scarcity of critical ones) is that it can affect the transition from a fossil-based energy system to one based on renewable resources, necessary to cope with climate change (Pommeret et al. 2022). On the same wavelength, Young et al. (2021) pinpoint in the Harvard Business Review site that in terms of the implementation of the corporate sustainable development goals, implementation of new solutions will inevitably trigger bottlenecks for the very resources, infrastructures, and capabilities upon which they depend. This danger springs from the fact that the rapid growth in the demand for raw materials, which are related to sustainability, will likely be much higher than the demand, something that at least will lead to a price increase for many of them (Young et al. 2021).

Supply chain disruptions, like the recent global pandemic, can inflict shortages of raw materials on supply chains, which can heavily test supply chain resilience (Amico et al. 2023), since they can create supply and manufacturing problems that supply chains might not be able to solve. The reason behind that is because such raw materials might be critical components of their end products.

Material risks can vary with the potential nature of the disruption (Althaf and Babbitt 2021). For example, when disruption led to price volatility or to a weakening of the environmental regulations, the risks in precious metals, like gold, platinum, palladium, were highly increased (Althaf and Babbitt 2021). But, when disruptions in supply chains led to supply pressures or to geopolitical tensions, the risk was higher for raw materials like cobalt, gallium, and key rare earth elements, as such metals are energy intense in terms of manufacturing, while their production is considered as highly geographically concentrated (Althaf and Babbitt 2021).

Another reason why scarcity in raw materials can heavily put under test the supply chain resilience is because such scarcity can increase raw materials' prices and can cause an escalation in global prices due to its shortage (Ayalp and Civici 2023). Such price increases can cause supply chain disruptions that test the resilience of our supply chain (Ayalp and Civici 2023), since companies, especially SMEs, might not be able to rebound economically or cope with the increased prices of the materials. This is something that might halt their production line, a situation that might be irreversible in some occasions. Resilient supply chains can tackle such cost issues. Either way, an increase in prices of raw materials can put pressure on supply chain professionals who need to figure out new ways on how to stay financially robust and to mitigate the increased prices problem without putting under pressure their supply chain resilience.

Cross Border Regulations

The global character and the complexity of supply chains today have brought supply chain professionals in front of many challenges, especially since they usually need to deal with cross-border situations, some of which can change any time and can create problems for supply chains' effective operations and harm their resilience and sustainability.One example of such situations is when different countries that are involved one way or another in international commerce and therefore are considered as parts of international supply chains impose tariffs. One well-known example of such a situation was when, in 2018 to 2019, tariffs were imposed on billions of products for U.S. importers, especially steel and aluminum, which led to import delays due to the inability of companies to adjust their current customs clearance programs toward absorbing the extra cost on their imported products (Katsaliaki et al. 2022). Such disruptions can lead to commerce failures, which can have a very negative impact on supply chain operations that might devastate the companies in question. If specific mechanisms are not in place to increase their reflexes and to help them rebound from such situations, their supply chain resilience might get a hard blow.

Therefore, supply chain professionals need to cope with such potential disruptions and to be ready to react because otherwise their supply chain resilience might be heavily tested with many adverse consequences for the whole company.

Although many can argue that international environmental regulations can have a positive impact on supply chain sustainability, thus resilience, there are some ways that such regulations might impose a negative impact on supply chain resilience. Such regulations might increase logistics costs, delay deliveries, potentially create problems based on embracing a sustainable supplier base, and so on. All these paragons that can be considered as the results of such regulations can heavily test supply chain resilience, since they will lower supply chain agility and will remove an important part of the company's available capital that might have been used in order to further support its resilience mechanisms, forecasting, contingency planning, data analytics, and so on. Therefore, although it is extremely important for such international environmental regulations to be in place, there is a concern that need to have specific and local characteristics as recent research in China has showcased (Xia et al. 2022).

Another situation that can test supply chain resilience in a hard way is international sanctions. Sanctions are specific measures that are imposed by the governments as a tool via which they can exert political pressure on another country or even punish it, and they are usually the result of actions from the opposed country that violated international norms or threatened national security (Tradecouncil.org. 2022). They are known in the form of, for example, trade embargoes, financial sanctions, arms embargoes, and so on (Tradecouncil.org 2022). Such measures can have severe consequences for the impacted country, while the restricted access to global markets and financial systems can hinder trade (Tradecouncil.org 2022), something which can negatively impact international supply chains and test their resilience.

In today's world, which is polarized in many ways, with two superpowers, the United States and China, involved in an "informal" contradiction, we have many examples that pinpoint exactly how crucial a role sanction can play regarding creating disruptions in global supply chains, which can create for example, scarcity of raw materials, a factor which as we discussed in 2.1 can heavily test supply chain resilience.

In July 2023, China imposed new export restrictions on gallium and germanium, which had a significant impact on other major economies like the United States and Japan, which use such raw materials in the production of high-end products, like advanced semiconductors and other military devices (eversheds-sutherland.com 2024). This move by China can be interpreted as a reaction to export restrictions that were imposed by the United States, Japan, and the Netherlands since late 2022, which limited the export of advanced computing and semiconductor manufacturing items to China (eversheds-sutherland.com 2024).

Likewise, in 2023, the United States imposed a new outbound investment restriction, which prohibited certain outbound investments by U.S. persons in "covered foreign persons" engaged in sectors that might pose a national security concern (eversheds-sutherland.com 2024). This restriction clearly targeted Chinese businesses, as "covered foreign persons" have been defined to include only specific persons who were in China (including Hong Kong and Macau). The targeted sectors included semiconductors and microelectronics, quantum information technologies, and AI systems (eversheds-sutherland.com 2024).

Such sanctions can disrupt local supply chains and when we are discussing some of the most powerful economies today, we can imagine the ripple effects that such disruptions might create in global economies. Such ripple effects can devastate smaller economies and companies and can test heavily their supply chain resilience, as scarcity in raw materials can create manufacturing deficiencies that might increase costs or even halt production, and therefore might make it quite difficult for many companies to overcome such problems and rebound, as they might not be able to overcome the scarcity of raw materials problem since no other suppliers of the specific materials might exist. This is a huge blow in their supply chain resilience, while there are no preventive measures that can help them recover from such situations.

Although it might seem that sanctions affect only one country, the one that is directly impacted by them, what usually happens is that, due to our globalized world, several other countries might be impacted as well, as sanctions can generate a ripple effect (Tradecouncil.org 2022). We will discuss about the ripple effect in the next chapter.

Workforce Shortages

The COVID-19 pandemic disrupted global supply chains in many ways. Companies suddenly needed to downsize their personnel and deal with new safety requirements, while in parallel, supply chain breaks and inventory shortages negatively affected manufacturing systems (Ambrogio et al. 2022).

In the last few years, after the pandemic era, a spike in retirements, in combination with a drop in analytical leaders entering the industry, created a lack in talented and skilled workforce in supply chains globally (Lebovitz 2021). This supply chain shortage is calculated to cause the loss of 2.4 million positions in the industry until 2028, causing a potential negative economic impact of $2.5 trillion (Lebovitz 2021). As a result, supply chain resilience and responsiveness are and will be put under severe test (Ambrogio et al. 2022).

It is evident that maintaining a full workforce is critical for supply chain-related operations and especially for port efficiency which of course affects in many ways the global maritime transportation systems, as well as the larger logistics systems and the industries these systems support (Li and Miller-Hooks 2023). For example, the chain reaction of events that can be provoked by an extended, large-scale absenteeism in one or more ports can affect the cargo-handling operations, competitiveness, and even the efficiency of international trade (Li and Miller-Hooks 2023), something that can also have a negative effect in global supply chains in terms of their resilience.

Recent research from McKinsey & Co highlighted the phenomenon of the after-COVID shortage in skilled workforce by bringing in forth the example of the United States, in which the demand for skilled labor has outstripped supply postpandemic (Bhattacharjee et al. 2021). In the case of the United States, the transportation and logistics sectors have been hit very hard, with severe impact on worker-retention challenges and rising labor costs that affected the whole supply chain of the country (Bhattacharjee et al. 2021). This shortage/mismatch in labor in the United States is depicted in Figure 2.1 in which we can see that the labor workforce is by 4.7 million less than it was prepandemic.

A safe result that can be extracted from the above is that supply chain resilience can be tested due to such shortages in skilled workforce, as supply chains cannot easily bounce back, especially after major disruptions, when there is no available personnel to put in the extra work needed during such challenging times.

Increase in Logistics Costs

In the volatile world that we are living in, one thing that can heavily test the resilience of our supply chains is the potential increase in logistics costs. Logistics costs can be influenced by several factors since global supply chains today are extremely complicated. The typical logistics costs for distribution logistics when handling customer orders can be divided into the following categories: warehousing costs for incoming goods, warehousing costs for storage of goods, fulfillment costs, shipping costs, and other logistics costs, which might involve, for example, returns (Waredock.com n.d.). Such costs have risen by at least 5 percent since 2010, mainly because of the increased complexity and rise of e-commerce logistics and the rise in the demand for faster fulfillment, while in parallel, we witnessed a demand for increased capacity toward meeting the rising demand (Waredock.com n.d.).

In addition, logistics costs can be influenced by the location and the level of development of the country in question, which of course impacts, for example, its infrastructure, economy, and so on. Therefore, for example, landlocked countries, especially developing ones, can face increased logistics costs, which usually are the result of poor road infrastructure (Arvis et al. 2010).

An interesting point here is that there is a connection between high logistics costs and low logistics reliability and predictability (Arvis et al. 2010), which can test the resilience of the whole supply chain as well, as supply chain professionals won't be able to forecast potential future logistics disruptions that might have an impact on the whole supply chain's resilience.

Exhibit 1

Labor mismatches have become prominent across the United States.

US job openings, index (Feb 2020 = 100)

US civilian labor-force participation rate,[1] %

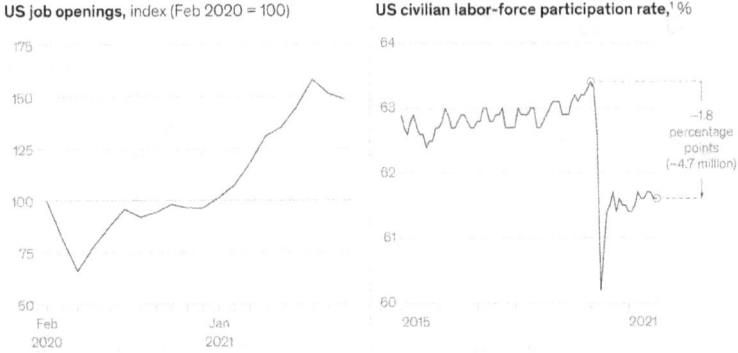

–1.8
percentage
points
(–4.7 million)

Job openings have risen beyond pre-COVID-19 levels
as the economy bounces back.

However, the labor force is about 4.7 million smaller than
it was prepandemic.

Source: Federal Reserve Bank of Philadelphia March survey; US Bureau of Labor Statistics

McKinsey
& Company

***Figure 2.1 Labor mismatches across the United States
(Bhattacharjee et al. 2021)***

An example that indicates how logistics costs can increase in our
globalized markets and put under serious test supply chain resilience
comes from the European Central Bank, which in its ECB Economic
Bulletin, in the 2021 issue, underlines that the increase in shipping
costs during that year was the result of two main things, namely, the
strong rise in demand for intermediate inputs on the back of stronger
manufacturing activity that raised the demand for Chinese exports and
the demand for container shipments and second, shortages in containers
in several Asian ports that created and even worsened supply chain
bottlenecks, which increased the shipping costs for Asian companies that
now had to pay a premium rate to get containers back (Ecb.europa.eu
2021).

Of course, the above example was the result of the COVID-19
pandemic, but it is the characteristic of how unforeseen factors can
affect the logistics costs of global supply chains, therefore can test their
resilience.

In general, companies try to "build" supply chain practices that can keep their costs low, including their logistics costs, but always calculating and acting under the prism of a stable business environment (Fiksel et al. 2014).

Several companies try to successfully face such problems. For example, the company Deere & Company, which is well known for its brand name John Deere, is famous for its manufacturing and supply of machinery used in agriculture, construction, and forestry as well as diesel engines and lawn care equipment (Byrne 2020). The company recently faced some supply chain cost reduction challenges as it was replenishing dealers' inventory weekly by using direct shipment and cross-docking operations from source warehouses located near Deer & Company's manufacturing facilities. This whole structure was not beneficial for the company as it was proven to be costly and too slow, so the company launched a program with the target of reducing its supply chain costs by 10 percent within four years (Byrne 2020).

The target was achieved via the redesign of its supply chain, which was based on the commissioning of intermediate "merge centers" and the optimization of cross-dock terminal locations (Byrne 2020). The company also started to consolidate shipments and use break-bulk terminals[*] during seasonal peaks, while it also increased its use of third-party logistics providers and, in parallel, effectively created a network that could have been optimized tactically at any given time. As a result, the company achieved an inventory decrease of $1 billion, a significant reduction in customer delivery time, which from 10 days went to 5 and an annual decrease in transportation costs of around 5 percent (Byrne 2020).

In that way, the company in question improved its customer service and decreased its logistics and overall costs, something that assisted it in getting more capital to invest in its supply chain resilience, while with the new structure, it became more agile, something that also

---

[*] Break bulk terminals: "Break bulk terminals are port terminals designed to consolidate or break up individual or bundled cargo and facilitate the overall break bulk shipping process. Break bulk cargo, such as grains, scrap, sugar, vehicles, beans, pipes, and similar goods are transported to these terminals via trucks or trains." (Gerrit n.d.).

increases its supply chain resilience as it can assist the company not overcome difficult situations and bottlenecks by avoiding, for example, interruptions in its supply chain logistics or to move merchandise in a quicker and efficient way when other companies might struggle under the pressure of the potential disruption.

Although there are companies like Deer & Company, which come up with a plan that can lower their supply chain/logistics costs and enhance their supply chain resilience, it remains a fact that disruptions can occur anytime and can inevitably increase, for example, logistics costs and not only. Different methods that try to keep logistics costs down, like just-in-time,[†] lean,[‡] and so on, can be proved inadequate and insufficient during crisis periods (Fiksel et al. 2014).

A very good and quite recent example of this negative turn in low logistics costs is the recent tsunami that hit Japan. Many companies that followed the lean inventory strategy were impacted by the tsunami hit, so companies like the General Motors Corp. in Colorado were temporarily shut down, while its Canyon plant in Shreveport, Louisiana, was shut down too due to the lack of crucial components that were supplied from Japan (Fiksel et al. 2014). Such incidents and disruptions not only can increase logistics costs but also can heavily test supply chain resilience. In our example, it is interesting to see how quickly and in which way General Motors managed to overcome the Japan tsunami hit crisis and so on.

Natural Disasters

Many natural disasters occur annually in the world. In the previous paragraph, we saw the example of the tsunami that hit Japan a few years

---

[†] Just-In-Time: "Just-in-time (or JIT) is an inventory management method in which you keep as little inventory on hand as possible. That means you don't stockpile products and raw materials just in case you need them—you simply reorder products to replace those you've already sold." (Stevens 2022).

[‡] Lean: "Lean is a way of thinking about creating needed value with fewer resources and less waste. And lean is a practice consisting of continuous experimentation to achieve perfect value with zero waste. Lean thinking and practice occur together." (Lean.org n.d.).

ago creating a ripple effect, which affected many overseas countries, like the United States, and so on.

Although specifically in Asia, natural disasters seem to have a much higher disaster ratio than in the Western world, all companies need to consider more carefully the negative effects that are associated with supply chain disruptions due to natural disasters, toward reducing their disaster risk and enhancing their supply chain resilience (Ono et al. 2015).

Major catastrophic events due to natural phenomena can disrupt economies far beyond local damage, as their effects can expand, even on a global scale, through supply chains causing uncertainty and overall chaos (Online.kettering.edu 2016). The most worrying part of the problem is that recent such disasters showcased that recovery could take even years (Online.kettering.edu 2016). Especially when natural disasters occur in rural communities, in which their economic survival heavily depends on the continuation, thus resilience of their supply chains, collaboration, vertical and horizontal, seems to be the key (Umar and Wilson 2021).

Individuals and families routinely receive critical for their survival goods such as water, food, medicine, power supply, fuel, and so on. All these are delivered via the efficient and well-operating global supply chains that the companies that provide those goods are using (Fema.org 2020). During the times of natural disasters though, even robust supply chains that were operating in a very effective and efficient way can be disrupted, something that can provoke acute life-safety challenges that can end up to a complete catastrophe with the loss of many lives (Fema.org 2020).

The risk of natural disasters that can disrupt supply chains is not confined by geographical boundaries, because negative effects can spill over, even globally throughout global supply chains and can affect all entities involved, like companies, governments, financial institutions, end consumers, and so on (Abe and Ye 2013).

It is not strange that supply chains need to enhance their resilience against the impact of natural disasters as the latter can heavily test it.

Recent research by Dudei et al. (2023) has revealed that companies throughout the world increase their investments toward building an enhanced supply chain resilience following disruptions due to natural disasters, as they understand that natural disasters can heavily test their supply chain resilience. The problem is that although many companies increase their investments toward the enhancement of their supply chain resilience, there are still many that are not that willing to take proactive measures that will help in tackling such phenomena and increasing their supply chain resilience. This is depicted in another recent research that showcased that the level of resilience preparedness, response and future plans that would have increased the overall supply chain resilience, vary among companies with different attributes, such as industry type and organization size (Maharjan and Kato 2023).

Human-Caused (Unnatural) Incidents

Events that can take place anytime in any place of the world like earthquakes, droughts, floods, and storms are considered as natural hazards, while unnatural disasters have to do with the deaths and damages that result from human acts (Sdgs.un.org n.d.).

Supply chains can face disruptions that can be natural, as we already saw in this chapter, but they can also be human-caused. Human-caused disasters can be human actions or decisions and they can include labor strikes, political instability, trade disputes, or even wars and cyberattacks (Intuendi.com 2024). Such events can lead supply chains to production stoppages, transportation delays, disruptions in communication and information flow, and so on (Intuendi.com 2024). Therefore, such incidents can heavily test supply chain resilience, so they need to be taken into serious consideration.

For example, political instability, trade wars, and international conflicts between nations can have severe consequences for global supply chains (Intuendi.com 2024). In addition, they can lead to tariffs and sanctions and other types of restrictions on the movement of goods, and therefore, they can disrupt global supply chains, while in parallel, they can significantly increase supply chain-related costs (e.g. logistics costs, etc.) (Intuendi.com 2024).

Other human-caused incidents that can test supply chains' resilience, might be, for example, glitches in the used software, cyber-attacks, critical system failures, supplier disruptions (e.g., suppliers' bankruptcies, labor disputes, quality issues, production delays, etc.), and transportation and logistics failures (e.g., port congestions, transportation strikes, infrastructure failures, etc.) (Intuendi.com 2024). Such events can disrupt supply chains, create bottlenecks, and can lead to even supply chain failures. Recent examples are the Ukraine war, the Gaza war, the Suez Canal bottleneck, or even, a bit older, the Chernobyl incident and so on, which led global supply chains into delays, bottlenecks, or even, in some cases, severe disruptions.

Other such well-known events that were human-caused include the tariffs imposed on billions of products for U.S. importers in 2018–2019, specifically on steel and aluminum, which led to import delays (Katsaliaki and Kumar 2022), or the Brexit in the beginning of 2020, which increased production failure risks to just-in-time auto manufactures and others that were involved in similar operations (Banker 2019, cited in Katsaliaki and Kumar 2022). Also, the civil war in Syria has created humanitarian logistics problems with refugee's flows in Turkey and in the European Union, which made supply chain professionals to change their approach from serving populations on the move, to serve dispersed but static groups of people by supplying refugee camps, and so on (Dudey et al. 2019b and c, cited in Katsaliaki and Kumar 2022).

We need not forget that, from time to time, economic downturns/economic crisis can heavily disrupt the global supply chains and test their resilience. Such examples include, but are not limited to, the huge economic crisis that was the result of the COVID-19 pandemic, which affected all supply chains around the world in a negative way and increased almost all supply chain-related costs.

Furthermore, the 2008 economic crisis had a profound effect on global supply chains of multinational companies and made them alter, maybe even permanently, some of their fundamental supply chain relationships (Mefford 2009), as the liquidity problems in the global markets, which started to interfere with global supply chains, created severe financial problems to important supply chain actors since, for example, most buyers and suppliers that were heavily dependent on their banks for liquidity suddenly faced important problems as their banks were not able to finance them as they started facing liquidity problems themselves (Mefford 2009)

Such incidents are extremely important as they can easily disrupt global supply chains, in the short and the long term, and put under stress test their supply chain resilience. Therefore, supply chain professionals not only need to take such potential events under consideration but also need to implement strategies, as we will see in Chapter 3, which will be able to mitigate such incidents and increase supply chain resilience.

What needs to be understood is that although sometimes unnatural events seem to have a local character, it is very common to take a global turn suddenly. This is another important reason why supply chain professionals need to always be ready to adapt to such events and to do their risk analysis to be able to take precautionary measures in the case that such events will develop a global character.

Shortages in Critical Components

In a global economy where companies from different parts of the world can be strongly connected and rely heavily on each other, shortages of specific materials/instruments/mechanical parts and so on, can become a huge problem for supply chain professionals and can heavily test the resilience of supply chains by causing severe disruptions.

For example, during the recent COVID-19 pandemic global crisis, shortages of ventilators for Intensive Care Units in the beginning of the crisis in many countries like, for example, in the United States, disrupted the health care supply chain with severe consequences in human lives (Dyatkin 2020). Local governments tried to find ways to alleviate the problem, but the fact is that international health care supply chains were not prepared for such high-scale disruption.

Another recent example was the 2021 semiconductor chip shortage which devastated the technology supply chain industry on a global scale (Hanbury and Hoecker 2021).

The above disruptions, which were the result of an unforeseen shortage in critical components, made, once again, even more pressing the issue of increasing supply chain resilience (Hanbury and Hoecker 2021). By the term "critical component" we mean components that are or contain ICT (e.g., hardware, software, firmware), which have been developed in a custom or commercial way and can be used in order to deliver or to protect the critical functionality of an overall system, or due to design of the system, may inflict vulnerabilities to the mission-critical functions of a system (Dau.edu. n.d.)

Critical components are also crucial in terms of their social impact. For example, cobalt, which is a critical component for lithium-ion batteries, can have a significant social impact due to its production geographical concentration in the Democratic Republic of the Congo (Althaf and Babbitt 2021). Therefore, for example, a natural disaster in this specific part of the world can create severe problems in cobalt production, which can heavily disrupt global supply chains, hence decreasing their resilience if they were not prepared for such disruption. This is another example of how something that seems to have a local character can suddenly become a global disruption and can put severe pressure on international supply chains' resilience.

Trust and Network Topology

One important element in supply chain management is trust. According to Giannoccaro and Iftikhar (2022), trust can positively affect supply network resilience. What is also interesting though is that topology is a factor that can influence the effect of trust on supply chain resilience in a positive or negative way (Giannoccaro and Iftikhar 2022). Continuing in discussing the results of their research, the above-mentioned researchers denote that centralized, diagonal, and hierarchical topologies can improve trust and accordingly resilience at a moderate level (Giannoccaro and Iftikhar 2022). On the other hand, in most local, small-world, block diagonal, and random topologies, trust is beneficial to supply chain resilience, while as the frequency of disruptions rises, the positive effect of trust on resilience decreases (Giannoccaro and Iftikhar 2022).

In general, it is well established that trust is a factor that can really test supply chain resilience in many ways. Research results point out that trust is extremely valuable in establishing supply chain resilience, especially when combined with digital transformation toward joint problem-solving (Faruquee et al. 2021). The role of digital transformation toward trust establishment between the actors involved in a supply chain is huge, while it can enhance trust that accordingly can enhance supply chain resilience (Faruquee et al. 2021).

In addition to the above, it is known that trust can be built upon the existence of communication and cooperation, two elements that can contribute to the enhancement of supply chain resilience (Mandal et al. 2018).

These results are important if we consider the ripple effect that can occur, which refers to disruption propagation across the supply chain that can affect its global performance and its resilience in the long run (Giannoccaro and Iftikhar 2022).

Therefore, it is evident that both trust and supply chain topology can test supply chain resilience and put it under vast pressure, especially during turbulent times.

The Ripple and the Bullwhip Effects

The ripple effect has to do with the impact of a disruption propagation on supply chain performance and the disruption-based scope of changes in supply chain structural design and planning parameters (Doldui et al. 2018).

In simple words, ripple effect refers to vulnerabilities and disruptions that, although they might be localized in a specific company, can lead to consequences that might affect the whole supply chain following a snowball course, and finally cause a resilience loss (Dolqui et al. 2020).

Some examples of the ripple effect are the following:

- The earthquake and tsunami that hit hard Japan back in 2011 disrupted multiple suppliers in, for example, automotive industry, something that continuously led to production breaks and material shortages all over the world (Ivanov 2018, cited in Dolgui and Ivanov 2021).

- Back in 2017, BMW's production was disrupted as the result of a supply chain shortage of steering gears, since BMW's first-tier supplier, Bosch, was unable to deliver the steering gears due to an Italian second-tier supplier experiencing production delays for certain steering parts, something that was the consequence of another event, which was internal machine breakdowns (Moetz et al. 2019, cited in Dolqui and Ivanov 2021).

- In 2020, the COVID-19 pandemic resulted in severe disruptions in production in many Chinese locations, while there were also missing deliveries from/to China that impacted the global supply chains and even the stock values of many multinational companies (Ghaffary and Molla 2020; Queiroz et al. 2020; Ivanov and Dolgui 2020a, cited in Dolqui and Ivanov 2021).

The bottom line is that a ripple effect can create severe supply chain disruptions as it can spread a local problem throughout the whole supply chain, something that, of course, can test the resilience of the whole supply chain.

Another well-known effect that can test the resilience of a supply chain is the bullwhip effect. The bullwhip effect refers to operational dynamics and amplify in the upstream direction, as ordering oscillations occur. downstream (Dolgui et al., 2020).

In order to understand how the bullwhip effect works, let's see the following example.

When selves are empty, retailers have the tendency to view that not as a temporary disruption, which, for example, might have been the result of a local or even due to a specific reason/event increase in demand, but instead as a permanent or semipermanent disruption, which they need to address successfully, and this is why they tend to overcorrect by placing orders for more items than they ordered before their selves were emptied (Pumilia 2022). Subsequently, distributors overreact as well by placing bigger orders with manufacturers to be able to cover the retailers, and in that way, they might even add 10, 15, or even 25 percent on top of the orders (Pumilia 2022). Consequently, and by having similar fears to face, even manufacturers overreact by churning out even more projects, as they strive to be sure that everything will be ok and that they will be able to cover potentially increased orders (Pumilia 2022).

As we can easily understand, this chain of overreaction of these different supply chain actors results in too much inventory, which is much less than the actual demand. As a result, retailers in order to sell excessive inventory decrease their price, move all excess inventory, or even worse, write off unsellable goods (Pumilia 2022). In any way, this can lead to major supply chain disruptions, which can heavily test the resilience of the whole supply chain.

Both ripple and bullwhip effects, as we saw, can create severe supply chain disruptions and can be another factor that can heavily test supply chain resilience.

Moreover, the two effects are strongly correlated, as the ripple effect can be seen as the bullwhip effect driver (Dolgui et al. 2020). The ripple effect can influence the bullwhip effect through backlog accumulation over the disruption time because of ordering of goods, which was not coordinated and due to production planning policies, that are in place (Dolgui et al. 2020).

Since, as we already saw, both the ripple and the bullwhip effects can play a negative role in supply chain resilience, it is important that supply chain professionals consider the risk that is imposed by both effects during the capacity disruption and the recovery period (Dolgui et al. 2020).

Notes for the Teacher

In this chapter, we discussed the factors that can heavily test the resilience of a supply chain, and we presented the most important ones explaining how they can test the resilience of a supply chain and result in a negative outcome.

Discussion Points

Some suggested discussion points are the following:

1. Discuss one by one the factors that can heavily test the resilience of a supply chain. Put the discussion into a global perspective and then discuss how the, for example, ripple and/or bullwhip effects can be a negative catalyst toward supply chain resilience.
2. Present a case study of the bullwhip effect. Split the students into groups and let them discuss their own case of a bullwhip effect.
3. A discussion can follow on whether such phenomena can be addressed by the companies. This can be a connecting link with the next chapter, which discusses the strategies that companies can implement to enhance their resilience. How doable is this? Which parameters are involved?

PART II

Every battle is won before it is fought   —Sun Tzu

CHAPTER 3

Supply Chain Resilience Strategies

Having a proactive strategy that can help you mitigate potential threats/ disruptions, especially during turbulent times, is extremely important. The importance of that is magnified today as disruptions in one part of the world can cause a ripple effect and affect another, e.g. oversees country. Being proactive and having the ability to "foresee" the next challenges/trends in the industry is a critical characteristic of the successful strategist.

In this chapter, we will discuss some of the most important supply chain strategies that can be used toward increasing its resilience in order to address potential threats and/or disruptions that might create problems in the proper execution of supply chain's operations.

Keeping an Inventory Buffer

Supply chain projects usually must face a certain number of uncertainties and mainly project activity time uncertainty and material consumption uncertainty (Kouvelis et al. 2023). What is also important here is that such activities might also be correlated, both positively or negatively (Kouvelis et al. 2023).

Also, in some cases, due to the nature of the product and the technology used by the involved logistics companies, certain other problems might occur. For example, in the supply chain of fresh agricultural products in China, commodity loses, which can be huge sometimes, usually occur during the transportation and storage of the products, mainly due to limitations in cold chain logistics technology, which can negatively affect the performance of the fresh supply chain (Li et al. 2019).

If, in situations like the above, one can also add fluctuations in customer demand due to unforeseen factors (e.g., a great recent example is the COVID-19 pandemic), or due to international incidents that can disrupt supply chains, thus the transportation of goods, one can understand that in supply chains which are based on the "push" philosophy, having an inventory buffer in place might be a great supply chain resilience strategy.

As everything in life, inventory buffers have their pros and cons while their implementation, is based on the overall supply chain strategy in question, as they are not needed when we follow a "pull" strategy or "make-to-order" approaches in production. Nevertheless, the pros of inventory buffers are risk mitigation, as they can reduce potential stockout risks, improved customer service, thus increased customer retention (on time in full (OTIF) service standards can always be reached), production stability, supplier reliability, as it can be seen as a safety net that can provide supplier flexibility when supply delays due, for example, to supply chain disruptions (e.g., blockage in the Suez canal etc.), can take place, and demand forecasting flexibility as it can absorb potential demand forecasting miscalculations (Lido.app. n.d.). In that way, supply chain resilience increases drastically, as it can overcome the disruption based on its, for example, inventory, which will assist it to provide its products to its customers even if, for example, the supplier's factory has been closed due to a natural or unnatural disaster and so on, and therefore no new products arriving at the company's premises.

On the antipodes of the aforementioned, the cons of holding a buffer inventory can be summarized as increased holding of goods costs, as companies need to maintain an inventory which never be needed, with all the attached consequences in insurance, inventory, and warehousing costs; reduced cash flow, since the cost of the buffer inventory could have been invested in another area that might have given to the company in question a, for example, competitive advantage, or have alleviated several other problems that the company might have been facing; risk of obsolescence, especially when we are discussing about sensitive goods that can become obsolete over time, like food and so on; storage constrains, since storage space is now being reduced due to the increased buffer storage; and potentially reduced efficiency, since over-reliance on buffer inventory can lead to complacency in improving supply chain operations, including production processes, something that over time might decrease the whole supply chain efficiency (Lido.app. n.d.).

Inventory buffers can be an important resilience strategy for many supply chains, although the above, potentially negative, consequences need to be taken under consideration. In addition to that, supply chain professionals need to have a holistic picture of the strategy that they want to follow as there is no "golden rule," or "one-size-fits-all." Therefore, inventory buffers need to be implemented only when they are fully aligned with "push"-related supply chain strategies, which also have their pros and cons.

Maintain Suppliers' Diversification

Disruptions in supply chain operations can happen anytime. Only in recent times several such examples come to our minds, like the COVID-19 pandemic, the Suez Canal blockage, the war in Ukraine and in Gaza, or, a bit older, for example, natural disasters, like the Japan tsunami and the Fukushima incident, and so on. Such disruptions can provoke huge problems in goods supply, which can negatively contribute to supply chain efficiency, customer satisfaction, and can create economic problems to the involved companies or might devastate societies that might be heavily dependent on those supply chains.

Imagine that such an event take place locally, like, for example, the Ukraine war, which devastated the country. What consequences might be for a company that is heavily, or even solely, dependent on suppliers only from this specific part of the world? The answer to this question is obvious and is an extremely negative one.

Many times, especially after the COVID-19 pandemic era, companies, in an effort to make their supply chains more resilient and to be able to cope with local disasters, tend to diversify their supplier base in terms of their location. Suppliers that are scattered in more than one area of the world can provide peace of mind to supply chain professionals who are trying to improve their supply chain resilience toward addressing, when needed, such negative local events.

The recent COVID-19 pandemic was a vivid example about why relying on a sole supplier or on suppliers from only one place in the world might be the basis for decreased supply chain resilience, efficiency, and customer satisfaction.

According to Larsen (2024), supply chain diversification is a specific strategy adopted by companies that focused on achieving resilience and agility in their supply chains. This strategy involves switching from relying on a single supplier or location, to working with multiple suppliers, not only for their goods' supply, but also for production (e.g., manufacturing) and/or services, in multiple locations.

Larsen (2024) also argues that sourcing from multiple suppliers, for multiple part or one only component or item, can greatly diminish supply issues, as if one supplier is unable to fulfil business needs, another supplier can step in to fill the gap, something that guarantees continuity and quick recovery from a crisis, thus increased resilience in the supply chain. But this is not only the case, as companies also use multiple locations for production, warehousing, and even sales in order to be able to avoid overseas disruptions that might hit them and would reach them due to the ripple effect (Larsen 2024). If this is the case, should one region experience issues in handling production, another region can produce to cover the gap in production (Larsen 2024). It is easy to understand that such strategy increases agility in the supply chain and of course continuity of production and most of all, resilience, as in this way the company can quickly overcome all problems and get back on tracks again as it can easily switch its production from one region to another and from one supplier to another.

Furthermore, supplier diversification can increase supply chain resilience in many other ways. Usually, it is connected to supply risk mitigation as we saw in the previous paragraphs. In addition, and according to Chod et al. (2019), supplier diversification can also be attributed to buyer risk. This is the case when suppliers are subject to buyer default and buyers might take costly action to signal creditworthiness to obtain more favorable buying terms (Chod et al. 2019).

The problem of this suggestion, according to the above-mentioned authors, is that when signaling costs are sunk, buyers sourcing from a single supplier can become vulnerable to future hold up, something that is somehow contradicting to the known quality of supplier diversification in terms of alleviating the holdup problem[*] (Chod et al. 2019). In any way, under this prism, supplier diversification can also enhance supply chain resilience even if it is seen via the lens of the buyers' perspectives and the holdup problem.

A very interesting example of the swift to supplier diversification strategies comes from Japan and specifically from Toyota, one of the biggest, if not the biggest, car manufacturer in the world. Traditionally, after World War II, Japanese companies based their supply chains on a model, which was called "Keiretsu." This model was based on obligatory relationships (Katsuki and Lennerfors 2013) between the central manufacturing company and its suppliers, all of which were local, in order, among other things, to ensure the swift delivery of parts, as companies like Toyota were based on the "just-in-time" model of manufacturing, which had as its prerequisite the collaboration with local/nearby-based supplier. In recent years, though, the Japanese giant, instead of buying exclusively from companies with which it had long-term relationships, also started to source from the global market, including mega-suppliers, because their streamlined operations allowed them to offer very low prices (Katsuki 7 Lennerfors 2013).

This swift in their business model allowed them to become more agile and to have a spread supplier base that ensured their supply chain resilience as now they were able to deal with, for example, potential economic "black swans" that might have devastated them in case they

---

[*] The hold-up problem: "Hold-up arises when part of the return on an agent's relationship-specific investments is ex post expropriable by his trading partner. The hold-up problem has played an important role as a foundation of modern contract and organization theory, as the associated inefficiencies have justified many prominent organizational and contractual practices" (Columbia.edu n.d.).

weren't able to be competitive, for example, in currency price fluctuations if they would stay connected only with local suppliers.

In addition to the above, in countries like Japan where natural disasters, like high magnitude earthquakes, tsunamis, and so on, can hit the country anytime, sourcing from different countries or even continents is a factor that can help in increasing supply chain robustness and resilience as the company can continue get the needed parts even when the local suppliers suffer from such disasters.

An interesting option, when supplier diversification is not possible for any reason (e.g., potentially low budget, etc.), comes from a paper titled "Capacity Investment in Supply Chain With Risk Averse Supplier Under Risk Diversification" by He et al. (2017). According to the authors, when a supply chain consists of one risk-neutral manufacturer and one risk-averse supplier, a risk diversification contract can be an option (He et al. 2017). According to that option, the manufacturer shares the losses of excess and inadequate capacity with the supplier, and under this prism, side payments can be transferred from the supplier to the manufacturer (He et al. 2017). In that way, supply chain resilience can also be enhanced to some extent, although supplier diversification is not achieved.

Supply chain resilience is extremely important, as we have seen till now, especially in some cases. The shift from single- to multisourcing in companies, which operate under an, for example, engineer-to-order supply chain strategy ("pull") and operate in an increasingly volatile, uncertain, and complex environment which partially is the result of their supply chain strategy, can highly increase their supply chain resilience (Mwesiumo et al. 2021). In such cases though, the implementation of a multisourcing strategy, although it can highly enhance supply chain resilience, it needs to be based on a purchasing and supply function right from the design stages, while it is essential such companies to be able to deploy some safety mechanisms to support their strategic decision, like, for example, a cloud-based procurement system that facilitates the interactions between the companies and their supplier base and combine that with the implementation of other critical organizational functions that might be involved in their projects (Mwesiumo et al. 2021).

The con that supply chain professionals need to have in mind when they turn to a supplier diversification strategy is that it might be proved quite difficult and complicated to build strong relationships with their suppliers, something that can be considered as a negative factor that can decrease the overall supply chain resilience. Therefore, if this strategy will be chosen, it might be good for the company in question to consider the communication and relations aspect and build on that by the implementation of, for example, a dedicated department that will have as its main purpose to focus on the long-term relationships of the company with its supplier base.

In addition to that, today's globalization made many companies to turn back to local-based suppliers as they started to be afraid of international incidents that might harm their, for example, sourcing strategic planning, as due to ripple effects negative incidents in a distant part of the world might affect their whole supply chain, so they suddenly changed their philosophy and started seeing localization in procurement as a safe and more easy to control approach. Also, in that way they tried to decrease their logistics costs. As we saw in Chapter 2, an increase on logistics costs can be a paragon that can heavily test supply resilience.

Back shoring and nearshoring are some of the results of this change in companies' strategies in these terms, as we are going to discuss in 3.3.

In general, supplier diversification is a strategy that can enhance supply chain resilience in many ways, especially in volatile environments like the one that we are living in nowadays, although supply chain professionals need to consider many other paragons, local and global when deciding to implement such strategy.

Consider Your Options Between Offshoring Nearshoring, Reshoring, and Back Shoring

The COVID-19 pandemic, which triggered global supply chain upheavals, shortages, and delays, forced many companies in the world to reconsider their supply chain resilience strategies (Stringer and Monserrat 2023) to be able to tackle similar future events.

Nearshoring, offshoring, back shoring, and reshoring are some supply chain strategies that have been used at a high extent by many companies around the globe in their efforts to optimize their supply chain operations.

According to Lip (n.d.), offshoring is a supply chain strategy that refers to relocating business operations, processes, or functions from one country to another, usually to a location that offers lower costs. In that way, companies strive to decrease costs while increasing their supply chain efficiency. It is not mandatory that all operations be relocated. Usually, companies choose to move certain operations, which are related to, for example, lower labor cost to help them to stay competitive in a global business environment (Lip n.d.).

On the other hand, nearshoring is a quite new phenomenon, which consists of relocating some previously offshored, usually manufacturing activities, to have them now close to previous core business locations, but not so close, because then they might suffer from deagglomeration[†] effects (Piatanesi and Arauzo-Carod 2019).

A good example of the situation is the "U.S. case." The U.S. response to COVID-19, supply chain wise, was nearshoring (Stringer and Monserrat 2023). Manufacturing was shifted from China to Mexico, something that resulted in the decrease of China's exports, while Mexico's exports surged, surpassing China by March 2023 (Stringer and Monserrat 2023). Proximity in that case significantly increased long-term supply chain resilience (Stringer and Monserrat 2023).

In addition to the previously mentioned, we also have another recent supply chain trend, which is called back shoring. The term "back shoring" encompasses relocations from either offshore facility, which is wholly owned, or from offshore suppliers to either own home facilities

---

[†] Deagglomeration: "The movement of activity, usually industry, away from agglomerations, perhaps when congestion makes further agglomeration in a region difficult and expensive" (Oxfordreference.com n.d.).

or home suppliers (Fratocchi et al. 2016; Stentoft et al. 2016; Wan et al. 2018, cited in Ancarani et al. 2019).

Another strategy that today is increasingly used toward the enhancement of supply chain resilience is reshoring, which can be defined as a company's decision to relocate activities back to its home country (Grappi et al. 2020). Reshoring has been also highlighted as a powerful supply chain resilience strategy from the study of Kazancoglu et al. (2024), especially in the manufacturing industry.

Reshoring and nearshoring strategies not only can be seen as responses, especially of manufacturing companies, against disruptions or unforeseen events (Andres et al. 2022) but also as strong determinants/strategies that can enhance their supply chain resilience. Resilience is strongly connected to sustainability, since coping with, for example, environmental challenges contextualizes the importance of resilience in sustainable development (Roostaie et al. 2019). A vivid example of this connection, which also highlights the importance of nearshoring and reshoring strategies in increased supply chain resilience via its contribution to the company's development, is the case of the Italian ceramic sector, as is depicted in the study of Andres et al. (2022).

According to that study, the supply chain for the Italian ceramic sector has been much benefited from nearshoring and reshoring strategies that reduced supply risk, while having a positive environmental impact. According to the same study, bringing extraction sources closer to facilities significantly reduces CO_2 emissions due to an optimal routing configuration as transportation distances now are shorter (Andres et al. 2022).

Nearshoring, reshoring, and back shoring can be seen as positive strategies that can enhance supply chain resilience, although one might argue that the localization that they bring might create problems in the case of a local natural or unnatural disaster.

But although all three strategies can enhance supply chain resilience, when it is time for a company to discuss which one is more suitable, the decision might be difficult. This is why we need to investigate a bit more the connection between these three solutions/strategies in order to pinpoint when it is better to use and which one is better to use for the character of a specific company.

One factor that needs to be taken into consideration is firm size. Firm's size directly influences the chosen alternative because larger companies prefer to nearshore instead to back shore (Merino et al. 2021). Therefore, for example, SMEs, which usually face specific challenges, as were discussed in 1.7., might be better to follow the back shoring strategy.

In terms of motivations, many might argue that the "made in" effect[‡] might influence the company's choice, but usually this is not the case at all (Merino et al. 2021). What really motivates companies to relocate back to their home country is the availability of skilled contractors and/or government's beneficial regulations (Merino et al. 2021). On the contrary, when companies are in fear of encountering barriers in terms of skilled contractors' availability and/or development of internal manufacturing competences, they usually prefer the back shoring option/strategy instead of, for example, the nearshoring or the reshoring ones (Merino et al. 2021).

In addition to the above, companies when choosing to return their manufacturing operations, for example, back to their home country need to consider other factors as well in terms of their supply chain resilience, like the locality of their, for example, suppliers or manufacturing facilities, and so on. Such a locality, although several years ago, could have been perceived as a paragon, which negatively influenced supply chain resilience since local natural or unnatural phenomena could have devastated the companies in question, as, for example, all their suppliers might suffered and even stopped their business. For example, imagine that all your manufacturing facilities are concentrated in one place only and, for example, a natural disaster soddenly hits hard this place, then suddenly there is a possibility that your manufacturing facilities will stop their production, so you won't be able to produce anymore. In

---

[‡] The "made in" effect: It is also called "country of origin bias" and describes a distortion that takes place, which influences customers and leads them to infer quality from only the product's country of origin (Dinnie 2004, cited in Diodato et al. 2018).

such cases, supply chain resilience will be extremely limited, and the companies in question, might even not be able to recover at all.

This decrease in supply chain resilience was always one of the reasons that drove companies to spread their operations among different parts of the world and go toward solutions like off-shoring. In recent years, though, there is a tendency for many companies to follow back shoring, reshoring, and nearshoring solutions because suddenly they started feeling like the need to be in control of their operations, especially since devastating international situations like the COVID-19 pandemic, the Ukraine war, the Gaza war, and so on. The fear of not being in control of their, for example, manufacturing facilities and that the spread of their operations on a global scale might decrease the resilience of their supply chain due to ripple effects made them to rethink solutions like the above.

So, companies are in need to take serious decisions regarding their supply chain resilience strategy/ies that they want to follow, as they need to take into consideration several factors that might be contradicting (e.g., having manufacturing facilities and/or suppliers spread in several global locations can increase the resilience of their supply chains due to unforeseen disasters, while on the other hand, such spread might lead to a loose control of their entire supply chain due to major negative international events, which might generate ripple effects that can heavily test the resilience of their supply chains).

Enhancement of Supply Chain Collaborations

As we saw in previous paragraphs, the COVID-19 pandemic era was a big "test" for many companies in the world in terms of how to operate their supply chains and how to increase their resilience, since suddenly they realized the importance of resilience in situations where nothing seemed to work properly. Therefore, since many countries implemented strict lock downs, the global supply chains were disrupted heavily as the flow of goods and/or raw materials was interrupted (Zeplin et al. 2021). As a result, many companies tried to reconfigure their internal and external supply chain networks and partnerships to support the resilience and efficiency of their supply chains (Zeplin et al. 2021).

In addition to the above, risk mitigation, which drives resilient supply chains, has become, in recent years, a priority for many companies as global operations have made supply chains more vulnerable to numerous risks (Zeng et al. 2017). Since companies want to enhance their supply chain resilience and since this enhancement goes through risk mitigation, companies became more inclined to form partnerships and engage in supply chain collaborations in a more conscious way (Zeng et al. 2017). The reason behind this strategic choice is that "two are always stronger than one," or in other words, companies started understanding that via collaborations they could be able to easier overcome potential supply chain disruptions and to recover in a quick way, hence, to enhance their supply chain resilience even more. This can be accomplished by sharing inventory, sharing suppliers, sharing knowledge and risk mitigation techniques, and so on.

According to a study conducted by Zeplin et al. (2021), supply chain partnerships, if based on the OTIF[§] delivery of materials and coping with potential changes in demand, can improve supply chain agility, resilience, and can create strong sustainable advantages for the companies in question. Especially in terms of supply chain resilience, OTIF can be a strong indicator (since it is a supply chain metric) of increased supply chain adaptability, something that is an indication of a very resilient supply chain that can adapt to crisis and recover quickly. The study concludes that supply chain agility can be a catalyst in enhancing supply chain resilience as it keeps the production process running normally and regulates production capacity, thus positively affecting the supply chain resilience (Zeplin et al. 2021).

Another recent research by Badwan and Nemer (2024) also highlights the importance of supply chain partnerships in improving supply chain responsiveness, resilience, and creating competitive advantage, since partners can be involved in work teams and exchange best practices (Badwan and Nemer 2024). The research also adds that the enhancement of supply chain resilience is also influenced by

---

[§] OTIF (on time in full): "OTIF is a supply chain metric that measures a supplier's ability to fulfill its delivery promises, meaning a customer receives exactly what was ordered, in the amount requested, at the correct location, and within the agreed upon timeframe" (Waters n.d.).

the company's capacity to respond promptly to variations in demand (Badwan and Nemer 2024), something that can be achieved via the implementation of the right partnerships as well.

The important role of partnerships in increasing supply chain resilience is also highlighted by Pratono et al. (2023), who underline that the turbulent global situation nowadays has guided supply chain leaders toward multiple partnership approaches (e.g., funnel-based and area-based partnerships, etc.), which allow supply chains to seize new market opportunities, address risks of professional misconduct, select partners for long-term collaboration (Pratono et al. 2023), and increase supply chain resilience.

The importance of implementing strong partnerships between key supply chain actors is also highlighted by another recent study by Cohen et al. (2023), which highlights that the top two key influencers of a company's approach in supply chain resilience are "homogeneity of internal supply chain processes and integration with other supply chain actors" (Cohen et al. 2023), which can be translated into the implementation of collaborative and productive partnerships.

Another research by Hida et al. (2022) combines the role of supply chain risk (SCR) mitigation and the implementation of strong partnerships with an increased supply chain resilience. The research underlines that the role of supply chain partnerships in enhancing supply chain resilience is increased when, and if, supply chain managers are also committed in paying the needed attention to SCR management, while it highlights that especially shipping companies that operate in the logistics industry need to establish supply chain partnerships and pool their resources due to their needs and exposure to others' techniques and procedures (Hida et al. 2022). Therefore, we can conclude that in addition to strong partnerships/collaborations, supply chain professionals need to also take additional measures which, for example, might be the right risk mitigation/assessment strategies.

Supply chain collaborations are a key point for increased supply chain resilience; when more companies collaborate in the supply chain, it becomes even more resilient (Lotfi and Larmour 2022). Furthermore, both horizontal and vertical collaborations between different supply chain partners are considered as strong determinants toward the enhancement of supply chain resilience, while it is also important that such relationships/partnerships/collaborations be based on a positive competition in the partnership, not in a negative one (Lotfi and Larmour 2022).

Therefore, collaborations, in general, can be a strong determinant toward an increased supply chain resilience, but this is not enough, as supply chain professionals also need to have an eye on SCR mitigation strategies. Moreover, the implemented collaborations need to be based on mutual trust and respect and on an ethical supply chain approach which will not be based on a negative competition, but instead, on a positive one, which will help all supply chain actors to excel, something that will also enhance the resilience and robustness of the whole supply chain.

Improvement of Supply Chain Visibility

Difficult situations sometimes require brave solutions. The globalized world in which we are living is imposing many challenges on supply chain professionals who are striving to increase the robustness and resilience of their supply chains. To achieve that, they try to use all the weapons they have in their armamentarium, especially everything that has to do with the use of new technologies.

One paragon that heavily affects supply chain resilience is the ability to see what is "going on" along each step/node of the supply chain. In other words, to have increased supply chain visibility.

According to Kalaiarasan et al. (cited in Swink et al. 2024), "visibility objects" are the types of data that companies make visible in a supply chain. What is interesting here is to notice that visibility-related data go beyond supply, inventory, and demand data that are usually used by the organizations and include product and process attributes in addition to insights into the specific supply network characteristics, structural linkages, and predicted events (Hall et al. 2013, cited in Swink et al. 2024). Supply chain visibility, which has access to this kind of data, can support potential planning and replanning processes, while it can be a catalyst in helping organizations anticipate potential future disruptions (Faruquee et al. 2021; Ivanov, 2020, cited in Swink et al. 2024), thus enhancing supply chain robustness and resilience.

Supply chain visibility and supply chain resilience are strongly connected. This was underlined in a research conducted by Brandon-Jones et al. (2014), which included 264 manufacturing plants and indicated that supply chain connectivity and information-sharing resources can lead to supply chain visibility capability, which enhances supply chain resilience and robustness (Brandon-Jones et al. 2014). The authors of that research also concluded that geographic dispersion, differentiation, and delivery complexity do not have contingent effects on the above-mentioned relationship between supply chain visibility, information sharing, and supply chain resilience (Brandon-Jones et al. 2014).

A very contemporary example of the importance of supply chain visibility in enhancing the resilience of its supply chain is the pharmaceutical industry. According to Stark and Zweig (2024), supply chain resilience is a priority for the pharmaceutical sector, while better supply chain visibility is considered a key strategy for improving supply chain resilience. The case with that sector is that pharma companies have complex upstream supply chains, while having low visibility into their suppliers' base compared to peer companies in other industries. This is the reason why companies in that industry need to take serious steps toward improving visibility, enabling more proactive supply chain management, reducing risk exposures, and as a result, increase their supply chain resilience (Stark and Zweig 2023), since increased visibility can enhance the ability to respond to shocks and fluctuations due to improved data availability and accuracy (Start and Zweig 2023).

The above findings are also supported by other studies. For example, a study conducted in Vietnam by Huang et al. (2023) also revealed that supply chain visibility significantly influences supply chain resilience. The interesting point though of this research, which took place in the garment manufacturing industry, was that beyond the aforementioned relationship, the research hypotheses that supply chain visibility and supply chain resilience have a positive impact on supply chain performance were rejected (Huang et al., 2023), something that needs to be taken under consideration from companies that might need to search deeper into the indirect relationships that may be mediated by factors, such as supply chain resilience and supply chain performance (Huang et al., 2023).

The correlation between supply chain visibility and supply chain resilience is also highlighted by another recent research, which was conducted in Malaysia between 154 electrical and electronics companies (Mubarik et al., 2021). According to that research, supply chain mapping is the mediating factor that enhances the connection between supply chain visibility and supply chain resilience (Mubarik et al., 2021). Adopting supply chain mapping strategies can improve supply chain visibility, which can then improve supply chain resilience, while visibility can also be increased by maintaining closer ties with key suppliers (Mubarik et al., 2021), something that also underlines the importance of partnership and collaboration in enhancing supply chain resilience, as we discussed in 3.6.

Another interesting parameter that can be an important determinant of supply chain visibility toward increased supply chain resilience is the magnitude of the digital capabilities of the company in question. Research, which was conducted in the health care industry (which is very sensitive in terms, e.g., of goods delivery, thus in need of increased supply chain robustness and resilience), between 137 respondents from the industry, found that supply chain visibility is a fundamental resource for digital capabilities (Tiwari et al., 2024). The main conclusion of that research was that these digital capabilities can be seen as a very important factor, which can enhance supply chain resilience, especially when companies operating amid highly turbulent environments (Tiwari et al., 2024).

An additional element that also need to be discussed here is that improving supply chain visibility, thus supply chain resilience, even via the route of supply chain mapping, requires the use of Industry 4.0[¶]

¶ Industry 4.0: "Industry 4.0—also called the Fourth Industrial Revolution or 4IR—is the next phase in the digitization of the manufacturing sector, driven by disruptive trends including the rise of data and connectivity, analytics, human-machine interaction, and improvements in robotics" (McKinsey.com 2022).

technologies, which include sensors that transmit information, which is then analyzed and synthesized in order to help us with forecasting or simply to help us increase the visibility by, for example, pinpointing the location of the products and so on. Therefore, we can say that the use of Industry 4.0 technologies can enable companies to develop and exploit their supply chain visibility toward enhancing their supply chain resilience.

The above signifies that companies of today that operate in dynamic global markets, and which wish to maintain their competitive advantage, need to upgrade themselves in terms of adapting into new technologies (Arvanitis and Hollenstein 2001, cited in Jain et al. 2024), as this adaptation can lead, as we have already seen, to an increased supply chain visibility and thus supply chain resilience.

In conclusion, we can argue that supply chain visibility has been proven as a paramount determinant that enhances supply chain robustness and resilience, especially for companies operating in highly volatile environments. The role of Industry 4.0 technologies and the level of digitalization of the company in question are also extremely important toward the enhancement of their supply chain visibility, thus resilience. These results are highlighted in many researches in different countries and industries and can be used as a springboard for informed decision making from supply chain professionals that can lead to an enhanced supply chain resilience.

Adaptation of Supply Chain Inclusivity

An interesting definition of inclusivity is that it is the "act of creating environments in which people can and feel welcomed, respected, supported and valued to fully participate" (Cority.com 2023). Such environments are extremely important since they embrace potential differences and offer respect in both word and action to all people involved (Cority.com 2023).

From the previous definition, we can understand that inclusivity is about respect, value, and involvement of all people in the processes and operations of an organization. The same goes with inclusivity in supply chains.

In this subchapter, we will discuss how supply chain inclusivity can be a catalyst in improving supply chain resilience.

Inclusivity in a supply chain has many faces, while its impact on it is high. Supply chain inclusivity can stimulate economic growth and job creation, especially in underrepresented communities, boost business performance via increased innovation and creativity as everybody is free to express his/her ideas, develop a better understanding and connection with customers, and improve reputation and brand image via the company's commitment to responsible business (Small business charter.org 2024).

In addition, it can enhance economic regeneration, as research from McKinsey & Company indicates, according to which, business with more diverse executive teams have 39 percent better financial returns (Small business charter.org 2024), while improving social impact, as inclusive supply chains support companies in ensuring that all potential suppliers have a fair and equal opportunity to compete for business (Small business charter.org 2024).

As we have already mentioned, a couple of paragraphs before, inclusivity in supply chains has many faces. One of them is inclusive purchasing, which is defined as "the ability of a buying company to manage social inclusion criteria" (Silva and Salomee, 2022). Such social inclusion can be seen as an important element of social sustainability (Silva and Salomee 2022). Inclusive purchasing is also considered an important factor in increasing supply chain resilience as it can amplify important supply chain resilience-related capabilities, like visibility, adaptability, collaboration, financial strength (Silva and Salomee 2022). Also, we need to never forget that companies with inclusive supply chains tend to recover quicker from crisis, thus to have increased resilience, as consumers seem to support such companies more, even during crisis periods, something that helps supply chains to not seize operations during disruptions.

This importance of an inclusive supply chain as depicted in its purchasing function (inclusive purchasing) in terms of enhancing supply chain sustainability and supply chain resilience is evident, while the existing literature highlights as well that it is scarcely used currently (Patrucco and Kahkonen 2021, cited in Silva and Salomee 2022) in supply chains. Such functions have been proven to be catalysts in supporting social sustainability as well.

All the above are indicative of the fact that inclusive supply chains can become a strong determinant of increased supply chain sustainability and resilience, as supply chain qualities like adaptability, collaboration, and financial strength can be further amplified via inclusivity implementation in supply chains, something that is proven to be a key element that enhances supply chain resilience (Silva and Salomee, 2022), as through disruptions, people need to be based on collaboration, and to be ready to adapt in order to rebound and return to previous operational status quo of their organization.

The huge impact of an inclusive supply chain in supply chain resilience is also highlighted by the fact that an inclusive supply chain is the one that instill in its employees a sense of belonging and commitment, while can improve morale and productivity, something that during turbulent times will make a huge difference in order to help the supply chain to return to its previous status (supplychain247 2024). In other words, it can be a strong determinant of supply chain resilience.

Finally, it is interesting to quote Andrea Hendrickx, county head —Germany in Infosys, who stressed the following: "By embracing a diverse and inclusive supply chain, organizations foster innovation, creativity and resilience. It brings with it a multitude of perspectives, ideas and solutions that can go towards addressing complex sustainability challenges" (Buchholz 2023). The above statement is indicative of the importance of inclusivity to supply chain resilience. Since all supply chain actors are welcomed and included in all processes, collaboration, communication, teamwork, innovation as ideas are free to move around, ethos via a culture of respect, sustainability can assist supply chains to tackle better potential disruptions and return to their previous status, thus to enhance their resilience.

Use of Supply Chain Data Analytics

Global supply chains are "exposed" to high amounts of data. The use of Industry 4.0 technologies can assist supply chain professionals to leverage these high data amounts towards different goals, including increased supply chain resilience.

The capability of a company to encapsulate the competitive advantage that can be acquired via the use of data analytics in its supply chain can be a very important paragon that can affect supply chain resilience. This can be the case especially nowadays, as data analytics, as part of the Industry 4.0 technologies that are implemented in the supply chain context, has gained increased popularity among supply chain professionals (Rezaei et al., 2022).

The interplay between supply chain resilience, data analytics, and supply chain flexibility is highlighted in a recent research by Rezaei et al. (2022), who denoted that supply chain resilience and organizational flexibility play mediating roles in the relationship between data analytics and the company's, in question, competitive advantage.

But is it indisputable that data analytics can be a factor that can positively influence supply chain resilience? Some, for example, might argue that institutional experience can be a factor that can positively influence supply chain resilience without leveraging data analytics. Nevertheless, recent research on the topic by Singh and Singh (2019) has highlighted exactly the opposite. In addition, the above research also underlined that if organizations adopt data analytics capabilities, they can be able to effectively utilize resident firm knowledge and develop the capacity to enhance their SCR resilience (Singh and Singh 2019). Such utilization of data analytics capabilities as part of the overall IT firm's capabilities has been proved to be a strong determinant of the company's risk resilience to supply chain disruption events (Singh and Singh 2019).

The connection between data analytics and supply chain resilience, which was introduced in the previous paragraphs, can be even more enlarged if we consider the complexity of today's global supply chains. On this basis, a study of 166 companies in the Pakistan area unveiled that not only data analytics is an important mediator between supply chain complexities and supply chain resilience, but also that it can be the catalyst toward structuring the existing supply chain complexities in a way that they can be harnessed by supply chain professional toward increasing their supply chain resilience (Iftikhar et al., 2023).

Supply chain resilience via the lens of data analytics can also improve the effective use of supply chain resources, something that can highly improve supply chain resilience (Zamani et al., 2023). Another important factor which can also lead to increased supply chain resilience; supply chain sustainability, can also be improved via the extensive use of supply chain big data analytics as it can lead to enhanced data-driven innovation (Piprani et al., 2023), which can also improve supply chain resilience.

Furthermore, other factors that can be combined with data analytics in the context of supply chains and toward the improvement of supply chain resilience are improvisation and anticipation (Munir et al., 2022). Such a combination can be paramount, especially during turbulent times of unforeseen disruptions and unexpected situations, as apart from supply chain resilience, it can also improve supply chain responsiveness (Munir et al., 2022).

Another important supply chain resilience determinant that involves data analytics is information quality. Data analytics in supply chains can increase the quality of the gathered data, while in parallel, it can enhance innovative capabilities (Bahrami and Sajjad 2022). Such results can enhance supply chain resilience and improve the overall supply chain efficiency in terms of operations.

One question that arises is that although it has been proved that data analytics are crucial in enhancing supply chain resilience, is their connection direct? Are other factors intervening, and if yes, what are they and what is their impact? Very recent research by Lee et al. (2024) highlights that the use of data analytics in a supply chain, especially in manufacturing firms, can be linked to flexibilities, which are related to supply chain resilience, but with a relationship which, against common belief, proved to be nonsignificant. The authors of that study underline that such findings are implying that companies that try to enhance their supply chain resilience also need to concentrate on their supply chain flexibility and that the company's data analytics capabilities should be faced as a prerequisite for increasing such flexibilities (Lee et al., 2024).

In addition to the above, supply chain resilience should not be left solely on the implementation of pure data analytics but also need to be based on an organization that demonstrates increased mindfulness and a humanitarian core (Dennehy et al., 2021). This is something that is extremely important if we want to implement ethical supply chains, which will not only be resilient and robust but also be able to be sustainable and to have a human-centric focus.

Finally, we also need to underline that the big data analytics in the supply chain management context are usually positively moderate the effect of supply chain ambidexterity on supply chain resilience (Xu and Liu 2024). This result is strongly connected to what we discussed in 3.4 about supply chain collaborations; although supply chain ambidexterity, which is "the simultaneous act of exploiting competences and exploring new opportunities" (Partanen et al. 2020), can decrease supply chain performance, network capabilities and strategic information flow with supply chain partners can be alleviating factors that can mitigate such a negative relationship (Partanen et al. 2020) and enhance supply chain resilience as well.

In conclusion, we can say that data analytics in a supply chain can be an important strategy, which, among other positive outcomes, can also enhance supply chain resilience. Again, though, we need to be able to use data analytics by simultaneously following a human-centric approach and by implementing an ethical supply chain culture that will be focused on the triple bottom line of our business.

Integration of Supply Chain Operations

Operations in a supply chain might involve many aspects of business, from procurement to sales and so on. All supply chain-related operations are extremely important for the proper functioning of all components of the supply chain and can affect its overall resilience.

Internal supply chain refers to that chain of activities that take place internally in a supply chain and can lead to the provision of the final product to the end customer (Basnet and Chuda 2013). Such processes involve multiple functions such as sales, production, distribution, and logistics (Basnet and Chuda 2013), as well as quality control, information sharing, collaboration, inventory management, and so on. The integration of all internal supply chain functions can be a catalyst toward the enhancement of the company's performance (Basnet and Chuda 2013).

The company's performance can also be enhanced via the enhancement of supply chain resilience, while supply chain integration in any form (supplier, internal, customer integrations) can be seen as the mediating factor between supply chain resilience and supply chain performance (Shen et al., 2023).

Therefore, it is safe to say that supply chain integration is strongly connected to supply chain resilience and supply chain performance, while the relationship between them can be influenced by factors such as industry type, national culture (e.g., power distance), logistics performance, and so on (Shen et al., 2023).

In addition to the enhancement of supply chain performance, integration and homogeneity of internal supply chain processes have also been proven to be very beneficial for the strengthening of the supply chain's resilience (Cohen et al., 2022). Of course, it is important here to emphasize that different supply chains have different resilience requirements, and therefore, different ways of achieving their resilience, while facing different obstacles toward that direction (Cohen et al., 2022), something that needs to be taken under consideration when companies striving to integrate their internal supply chain processes toward increasing their overall supply chain resilience.

The positive role that supply chain integration has in supply chain resilience usually passes through agility and supply chain robustness, which is also positively influenced by supply chain agility (Zhuo et al., 2021). This fact per se means that supply chain stakeholders should efficiently exchange information in order, via collaboration, to jointly make plans toward enhancing the resilience of the supply chain in question against potential threats and risks (Zhuo et al., 2021). What is crucial in this case is the role of another important stakeholder, which is the government, and which needs to play the role of an efficient policy maker, which encourages and facilitates potential supply chain integrations that might take place among supply chain members to enhance supply chain resilience (Zhuo et al., 2021).

The positive role of supplier, internal, and customer integrations in enhancing supply chain resilience is also highlighted by a recent research that was conducted in China by Qi et al. (2023).

Although this connection is strongly evidenced by this and many other researchers, there might be a very beneficial development of a contingency framework via which the supply chain integration–supply chain resilience connection should be examined (Qi et al., 2023). Such a framework might cover aspects that potentially might affect that relationship, which should be addressed properly.

Finally, in research, which was conducted in China between 273 Chinese companies, the findings suggested that two other parts of supply chain integration: information and service integrations, are also positively correlated to supply chain resilience, while transaction integration was found to not have a substantial correlation with supply chain resilience (Wu et al., 2023).

In general, we can safely argue that integrating important supply chain operations and key stakeholders can be a decisive factor that can alleviate serious supply chain malfunctions and can fortify supply chains by increasing their robustness and resilience. In addition, it might be very useful to implement a framework that will assist supply chain professionals to better address everything that has to do with the correlation between supply chain integration and supply chain resilience and to more thoroughly investigate potential other parameters that might affect that relationship.

Use of New Technologies

Three aspects of supply chain management that are strongly connected are supply chain finance (SCF), SCR, and supply chain resilience. SCR information processing capabilities can have a quite significant impact on both SCF and supply chain resilience (Yaqin and Li 2022). The role of SCF between the other two aspects is a mediating one, while environmental uncertainty moderates the relationship between SCF and supply chain resilience (Yuan and Li, 2022). In addition to the above, the role of the use of new technologies in enhancing supply chain resilience is highlighted by many studies, while firms today strive to leverage their use and apply them in their supply chains to improve collaboration, visibility, efficiency, transparency, and resilience.

The application of new digital technologies that came with Industries 4.0 and 5.0 can be seen as a decisive factor in terms of facilitating the optimization of supply chain alignment, stabilization of the supply–demand connection, provision of supplier innovation capabilities, and so on, factors that can enhance supply chain resilience as well (Rui and Bao 2024, cited in Huang and Ping-Kuo 2023).

What we need to underline here though is that both experience and existing literature indicate that Industry 4.0 technologies do not have a direct impact on supply chain resilience, but instead, their implementation enhances specific resilience-related elements like flexibility, redundancy, visibility, agility, collaboration, robustness, and information sharing, as we will see in the following paragraphs (Marinagi et al., 2023).

Since, both supply chains and manufacturing systems robustness and resilience are key parameters needed to ensure reliable and efficient production processes, their facilitation, which is urgent now more than ever due to the continuous disruptions that we globally experiencing, can be assisted by the use of Industries 4.0 and 5.0 technologies (Sesana and Tavola 2021). This is why supply chain professionals need to integrate in their already sophisticated IoT and artificial intelligence (AI)-based systems, which assist them to monitor and detect critical situations, new technologies like augmented reality, virtual reality, and so on, that can assist them to make informed actions on a bidirectional continuous connection (Sesana and Tavola 2021).

One of these new technologies is Metaverse, which is a three-dimensional digital world and has many benefits, especially in promoting collaboration among supply chain actors and strengthening relationships, factors that as we have already discussed are powerful enablers of supply chain resilience (Huang and Ping-Kuo 2022), assisted also by factors such as sensory feedback and so on (Huang and Ping-Kuo, 2022).

Metaverse technologies when implemented in a supply chain context can not only improve trust and collaboration among supply chain actors but also can enhance knowledge sharing and adoption behavior via the use of sensory feedback, factors that again increase supply chain resilience (Chen et al. 2023).

The use of Metaverse technologies creates a chain reaction when implemented in a supply chain. As it can create a sense of physical proximity, it can influence firms' emotional attitude during interactions, facilitate feedback via sensors, and therefore strengthen emotional expression, something that assists supply chain professionals to adapt rational behavior toward taking decisions of mutual trust (Chen et al., 2023). The establishment of this trust helps in promoting green knowledge sharing and strengthens supply chain resilience (Chen et al., 2023).

Another new technology that can be used toward the improvement of supply chain resilience is Digital Twins. Digital Twins when implemented can assist supply chain professionals to monitor in a more effective way potential disruptions, event-driven responses, learning, proactive thinking, while it can be used as a strong supporter of the integration of proactive and reactive approaches to supply chain resilience which leads to its enhancement (Ivanov 2023).

Supply chain professionals can simulate situations and see how specific elements of their supply chain could have reacted under specific disruptive circumstances. Therefore, supply chain professionals can be prepared when crisis will hit, something that can increase the resilience of their whole supply chain.

Digital Twins technology can be seen as a facilitator toward making the unknown known and as a contributor to the development of a proactive, adaptation-based view on supply chain resilience and viability (Ivanov 2023). Digital twins can be used in several ways in a supply chain, for example, in production systems, warehouses, distribution networks, and so on, and guarantee adequate levels of supply chain performance (Longo et al. 2023); therefore, they can attribute positively in an increased supply chain resilience. Especially in industries like the semiconductors one, where data are rich, deploying simulations via the use of digital twins is a practice that has already begun with rich results in the analysis of supply chain resilience (Nguyen et al. 2023).

Another important new technology that professionals use today in their supply chain is AI, which can be used as part of the Industry 5.0 technologies in manufacturing, supply chains, decision making, and so on. What we need to underline here is that we also need to acknowledge the importance of the use of AI as a strong determinant of the enhancement of supply chain resilience. In addition, that relationship between AI and supply chain resilience can be mediated using dynamic capabilities and open innovation (Le and Abhishek 2024). Therefore, when disruptions occur, the importance of AI, as a strategic tool for companies to improve their supply chain resilience via the path of the increase of their dynamic capabilities, is paramount (Le and Abhishek 2024).

Moreover, AI can contribute in several ways in enhancing supply chain resilience. It can enhance transparency, it can ensure the efficient and secure last-mile delivery, it can offer personalized solutions to both upstream and downstream supply chain actors, it can minimize the impact of potential disruptions, it can facilitate an agile procurement strategy (Modgil et al., 2022). All the above are decisive enablers of an increased supply chain resilience, since during crisis, a supply chain that can offer agility, efficient delivery, and transparency can not only be very responsive no matter the circumstances but also can rebound quickly as it can find new ways to overcome disruptions and can continue operations on a more stable way.

Other technology that can enhance supply chain resilience is the use of internet of things, which can enhance real-time monitoring of raw materials and finished goods, while in that way it can enhance supply chain's network responsiveness and efficiency (inboundlogistics.com 2024). This can be done via the use of sensors that can track critical goods across the supply chain, and in that way, they can significantly reduce risks that are associated with transporting and storing sensitive materials (Inboundlogistics.com, 2024). Also, via the use of sensors, supply chain visibility can be enhanced, something that can have a positive impact in supply chain resilience as it can improve the operational efficiency of the company during crisis, can pinpoint the location of its products while moving, and therefore can adjust its movements in terms of inventory and orders, something that can also increase efficiency.

Furthermore, the use of blockchain technology can be decisive in terms of strengthening economic security while enhancing trust among supply chain actors (Inboundlogistics.com 2024). Smoother and more reliable exchanges between different supply chain actors and fortified trust can enhance supply chain resilience as in difficult times all supply chain actors can collaborate, since there such collaboration can be based on the enhanced trust that was built via the use of blockchain technologies in the supply chain, while economic downturns can be avoided via the implementation of a smooth and secure transactions system via the use of blockchain technologies (Inboundlogistics.com 2024).

Other new technology that can be used by supply chain professionals toward the enhancement of supply chain resilience can be cloud computing that supports supply chain networks in adapting to the climate change impact via the enablement of global data accessibility and collaborative resilience planning (Inboundlogistics.com 2024); therefore, it can enable the enhancement of supply chain resilience via uninterrupted data flow and collaboration schemes between supply chain actors, which during crisis can assist toward the quick recovery of the supply chain.

The use of advanced analytics can also increase supply chain resilience by providing insights that can assist companies in terms of anticipating potential disruptions in their supply chain, something that can help them in adjusting their strategy and enhance their supply chain resilience (Inboundlogistics.com 2024).

In general, many new technologies can be used today from supply chain professionals to help them increase supply chain performance, robustness, and resilience. Their use usually does not have a direct impact on supply chain resilience, but it has an indirect one, as it impacts different mediating factors that then influence supply chain resilience.

Implementation of Supply Chain Ambidexterity and Risk Management

Developing a resilient strategy for organizations today is extremely important as they must deal with major disruptions. Such strategies will help them to survive during turbulent times, to adapt and to grow by developing their competitive advantage (Munir et al., 2024).

In a quite extensive research, which was conducted by Munir et al. (2024), which involved 406 supply chain professionals in different product-based industries in Pakistan, Bangladesh, and India, the results highlighted that ambidexterity and risk management have a substantial positive impact on supply chain resilience, while the paragon, which had a mediating and connecting effect on them, was the supply chain analytics one (Munir et al., 2024). In this chapter, we had already a short discussion on what ambidexterity is in supply chains and how this is connected to risk management and supply chain resilience. These results are indicative of the fact that the employment of supply chain strategies that can utilize existing capabilities combined with practices that spring from experienced supply chain professionals toward developing and/or explore new skills to be applied in the existing supply chains can significantly impact supply chain resilience, while such ambidexterity in supply chain can be effectively supported by the implementation of supply chain analytics (Munir et al., 2024), which will also enhance the decision making in terms of risk management.

Although as we have already discussed, supply chain ambidexterity can downsize supply chain performance, it is an important positive factor that can enhance supply chain resilience with the use of efficient information flow, networking, and data analytics. Supply chain ambidexterity can increase efficiency without compromising flexibility, something that also increases agility and therefore makes supply chains more ready and capable to respond to crisis since they are agile.

But what about SCR management? Is it that important as well? In a study conducted in France between 470 French companies, the results indicated the strong connection between SCR management and supply chain resilience (El Baz and Salomee 2021).

The importance and the interrelationships of the elements involved in SCR management, resilience, and reliability are also highlighted in a study by Bo et al. (2023), which was conducted in Norway. Such interrelationships can be proved not only valuable, but also extremely important in enhancing supply chain resilience during turbulent times.

In general, it can be argued that there are numerous studies that investigate the correlation between SCR management and supply chain resilience (Silva and Salomee 2022).

Simba et al. (2017, cited in Silva and Salomee 2022) supported the idea that SCR management, including risk detection, risk valuation, risk moderation, and risk checking can be a catalyst toward increased supply chain resilience.

The effect of SCR management practices (including flexibility, collaboration, and redundancy), on supply chain resilience via the enhancement of supply chain flexibility and collaboration, was also highlighted by Zineb et al. (2017, cited in Silva and Salomee 2022).

On the same wavelength, the vice versa approach was underlined in another study conducted by Saglam et al. (2020, cited in Silva and Salomee 2022), as the researchers pinpointed a strong effect of supply chain responsiveness and resilience on supply risk management performance.

Therefore, we can argue that two important supply chain strategies that can enhance supply chain resilience are the implementation of ambidexterity in a supply chain in combination with information flow, data analytics, and networking and the implementation of risk management mechanisms that will increase supply chain flexibility, collaboration, and redundancy.

Investment In Reskilling and Upskilling

As we have already discussed in Chapter 2, skilled employees' shortage is a vast supply chain problem nowadays, which tests supply chains' resilience. Companies all around the world are trying to find solutions to that problem, with the most used ones to be automation, outsourcing, reskilling and upskilling.

Reskilling and upskilling in our ever-changing world are extremely important. Indicative of that is what the World Economic Forum underlines "As jobs are transformed by the technologies of the Fourth Industrial Revolution, we need to reskill more than 1 billion people by 2030" (Zahidi 2020).

The technological evolution that industries 4.0 and 5.0 have brought can help industries to evolve, which means that the evolvement of the workforce also needs to take place in order employees to be able to cope with that evolution (ASCM.org 2020). Supply chains must contend with many technological and systematic advancements (ASCM.org 2020) that are also discussed in this chapter and can affect supply chain resilience.

Industries evolve with technology, and that means the workforce needs to evolve as well. Supply chain is no exception. Reskilling and upskilling are two commonly used approaches by supply chain companies today as they are focusing on their existing employees without the need for outsourcing or hiring new ones. Upskilling refers to the process of learning new skills or teaching workers new skills that will help them in their respective position, while reskilling refers to the process of learning new skills so they can do a different/new job (Microsoft.com 2023). So, it can be said that both reskilling and upskilling can optimize productivity and efficiency across the supply chain (Levis 2021).

By optimizing productivity and efficiency and by having a workforce that is up to date regarding all new technologies that are implemented in a supply chain, supply chains can enhance their resilience as during crisis situations that workforce can be the catalyst toward overcoming the crisis. The reason behind that is multiple, as upskilled and reskilled employees not only have self-confidence regarding their competencies, something which is vital toward recovering from crisis, but also they will be a strong determinant in terms of how supply chains will survive and rebound through the use of new technologies.

The aforementioned paragraphs highlighted the importance of upskilling and reskilling for supply chain resilience. Their role is multiple, but especially in turbulent times, both upskilling and reskilling have a significant effect in supply chain resilience (Edeh et al., 2020), since they can "upgrade" the existing supply chain workforce and help the whole supply chain to rebound after a negative event that might disrupt it.

Implementation of Sustainability Strategies

There is an interplay between supply chain sustainability and supply chain resilience. They are both considered to be two different concepts, which have separate and distinguishable goals (Carissimi et al., 2023). Resilience can be seen as a component of sustainability, while sustainability can be seen as a component of resilience; therefore, they are considered by many as synonyms (Carissimi et al., 2023). This is mainly because a sustainable supply chain means that it guarantees a future in terms of societal., environmental, and economic paragons that are involved. If all the paragons are stable and strong, the supply chain in question can easily navigate a crisis and overcome it quickly as it has the mechanisms in place that would continue to guarantee its future under the triple bottom line prism.

An interesting element though is that some supply chain managers perceive their relationship even as a conflictive one, while others as synergistic, and some even see them as fundamentally orthogonal to each other (Cotta et al., 2023).

Furthermore, a recent study by Negri et al. (2021), has concluded that the relationships between supply chain sustainability and supply chain resilience are often incoherent since they pinpointed a confusion between sustainable and resilient supply chain practices with no clarity on how such processes could help them both to advance together (Negri et al., 2021). Moreover, the authors of that study underline that there exists a major conflict between the two concepts since sustainability generally focuses more on efficiency, while resilience can be said to mainly focus on effectiveness (Negri et al., 2021).

This interplay between the two concepts highlights their strong correlation. What is certain is that although they might be different concepts, different sustainability strategies can influence supply chain resilience in several ways. For example, cleaner production can influence supply chain resilience by having a positive impact on both economic and social issues (Aming'a et al. 2024), which in the long run can increase resilience since a company with strong economic pillars is easier to withstand and absorb strong hits during a supply chain disruption.

Also, green procurement strategies combined with long-term environmental plans/designs can increase environmental sustainability and in combination with, for example, reverse logistics, can have a positive impact on supply chain resilience (Aming'a et al. 2024). This can happen because such plans/designs can create a very positive social grip that the company now developed, which enhances its connection to the society and can increase possibilities for collaborations between actors in the supply chain, the government, and consumers. That can assist the company during crisis to get all the help it can get and to rebound quickly.

The positive relationship between sustainable strategies and supply chain resilience is also highlighted in several researches like the one by Ali et al. (2024), which also underlines the need for more resilient supply chain networks for increased sustainability, while emphasizes the role of digital technologies in promoting sustainability via the enhancement of environmental controls toward supply chain efficiency (Ali et al. 2024), which can lead to increased supply chain resilience.

Organizational sustainability needs companies to act toward social responsibility and an increased positive environmental impact (Rostam-zadeh et al. 2018, cited in Han et al. 2024), while implementing sustainability strategies is recognized today as a very important strategic approach that companies can adapt to cope with today's challenges and uncertainty in global markets (Giannakis and Papadopoulos 2016, cited in Han et al. 2024). Therefore, since sustainability is extremely important and a major strategic approach for the companies of today, they also need to address sustainability risks and lessen their impact, as in that way they will be able to also achieve the increased supply chain resilience that they need (Giann akis and Papadopoulos 2016, cited in Han et al. 2024). This is why supply chain professionals need to adapt the appropriate risk mitigation strategies to cope with potential supply chain sustainability risks toward the improvement of the overall supply chain resilience (Giannakis and Papadopoulos 2016, cited in Han et al. 2024).

As we can see from what has been discussed in 3.14, several aspects like supply chain sustainability, risk mitigation, and supply chain resilience need to be combined to increase what we call supply chain survivability, which has to do with the need to find a new temporary equilibrium during turbulent times that will assist supply chains to survive (Korchi and Akram 2022).

In a world that needs to become more sustainable and in which companies adapt more sustainable strategies, the classical resilience capacities (e.g., absorptive, adaptive, restorative, etc.) are not enough anymore to deal with sudden, high-impact disruptions like the COVID-19 pandemic (Korchi and Akram, 2022). Therefore, supply chain resilience needs to incorporate survivability via the use of enhanced supply chain sustainability strategies, especially during highly impact disruptions.

Globalization and new technologies in combination with the complex nexus of manufacturing, logistics, and retail companies nowadays make it extremely significant for companies, no matter the industry in which they operate, to implement supply chain sustainability and supply chain resilience-related practices (Paul et al., 2023).

Sustainability practices can positively enhance supply chain resilience, while the opposite is also possible (Michel-Villarreal 2023). What is extremely important, especially after humanity's experience with the COVID-19 pandemic, is that social sustainability practices in supply chains need to be on the spot, as they not only have so much to offer to societies, but also because they are considered, and not without a reason, as enablers of supply chain resilience capabilities (Michel-Villarreal 2023).

Sustainable practices in supply chains include all aspects of the triple bottom line, namely, people, planet, and profit. A supply chain, which takes under serious consideration these three aspects and tries to enable and support them via the use of sustainable strategies, can be in a position that not only will potentially acquire the competitive advance that was always looking for, but it will also be able to guard with safety its future. This fact per se is enough to increase its resilience, especially when it is tested by disruptions that have a negative impact in its supply chain.

Enhancement of Supply Chain Cyber Security

As we have already discussed in this chapter, supply chains to enhance their resilience and, in general, to improve performance and efficiency implement strategies that are based on digitalization via the use of new technologies that came with industries 4.0 and 5.0. This vast digitalization of supply chains sometimes comes at a cost. Cyber security threats are spreading, and supply chain professionals know very well that they need to be ready and able to tackle such threats that might impose high risks in supply chain operations. Resilience, sustainability, and cyber security are three measures in supply chains that are used to define how robust a supply chain is and whether it can operate/perform without disruptions (Hossain et al. 2023).

The role of cyber security in the enhancement of supply resilience is extremely important, especially nowadays. Efforts from organizations from all over the world have come to support that and to facilitate the implementation of cyber security practices toward the enhancement of supply chain resilience. For example, the IBM Institute for Business Value, partnered with Microsoft to shed some light on how cyber security factors can shape supply chain resilience (IBM.com n.d.). The results were depicted in a recent report of a global survey of 2,000 cross-industry security and operations executives. The findings of this report highlighted that only 30 percent of respondents prioritized a secure, connected supply chain ecosystem in their operations (IBM.com, n.d.). In addition to that, the results indicated that managers who were able to see cyber risks and SCR as connected and intertwined were the ones who had to face the less disruptions (IBM.com, n.d.), thus putting less strain on their supply chain resilience, since they were able to easily mitigate those risks via a holistic risk management approach, which can be considered as a proactive strategy toward increased supply chain resilience, as risk-free supply chains are easier to rebound from a crisis since they have to deal with less risks and uncertainties.

Such findings underline the important role that cyber security has toward an enhanced supply chain resilience if being seen in the context of a supply chain ecosystem. They also denote that a strong, shared security culture across suppliers and other important supply chain actors, which are less exposed in cyber threats can increase resilience for the whole supply chain (IBM.com, n.d.).

Seeing supply chains as an ecosystem, which needs to be protected from external threats and disruptions, is crucial in establishing a powerful framework that will strengthen cyber security across that ecosystem and will result in an overall resilient supply chain. In order such ecosystem's cyber security to be achieved, there is a need for raising risk awareness, standardized policies, collaborative strategies, and empirical models to be implemented among all actors involved in the supply chain ecosystem in order to increase supply chain resilience (Ghadge et al. 2020).

Lack of cyber security awareness as it was pinpointed in the above-mentioned IBM report is a very negative factor when addressing critical gaps in the managerial decision making of supply chain officers, especially at the executive level (Muller, 2022). The problem is usually, as research has shown, that supply chain executives tend to not handle cyber security as a potential threat to their supply chains (Muller, 2022). Collaboration and integration in supply chain ecosystems seems to be the solution for an enhanced supply chain resilience, especially on the digital level, while cyber SCR management strategies need to go beyond single companies and need to be seen in a more holistic way including all ecosystem actors (Muller 2022).

As a result, one can argue that supply chain cyber security strategies not only need to be implemented by supply chain professionals but also need to be seen from a holistic way that include all relevant supply chain actors and see supply chains as an ecosystem. In that way, supply chain resilience can be increased for all involved actors, something that can have positive consequences that can positively affect supply chains and the society as a whole.

Implementation of an Ethical Supply Chain

Globalization has led to an exponential growth of international business, something that makes even more important to start focusing on ethical business practices, while negotiations, as a critical component of international business, become even more essential (Alexander et al. 2019). Therefore, implementing an ethical climate across the supply chain echelons can be a crucial paragon for its sustainability and resilience.

The implementation of an organizational ethical climate can be a decisive paragon that can positively influence crucial operational elements, for example, information security in a supply chain, which can be strong enablers of increased supply chain resilience (Tan et al. 2022).

In addition to the above, ethical purchasing management has been highlighted in recent years as an important factor that can strengthen supply chain resilience since it can safeguard organizations from being "accused" by their stakeholders for irresponsible/unethical behavior (Goebel et al. 2012). Such ethical purchasing management should be based on a more socially and environmentally sustainable and ethical supplier selection, something that is also connected with supply chain governance, as it can give the direction toward a more social and environmentally sustainable way that purchasing managers need to choose their suppliers (Goebel et al. 2012). Such purchasing strategy can be the catalyst toward a sustainable supply chain, and as we already saw in this chapter, a sustainable supply chain can impact its resilience in a very positive way.

In general, the corporate culture that is implemented through the supply chain in addition to social responsibility practices from the supply chain actors and their combination with the right leadership tactics are crucial elements that can characterize the ethos of a supply, while they can have a positive impact on supply chain resilience

(Chen et al. 2023b). Such elements are interconnected as, for example, corporate social responsibility can positively influence corporate culture and values and leadership (Chen et al. 2023b). In addition, such elements can have a positive impact in supply chain resilience and their implementation from supply chain organizations can be a very positive strategy.

But what do we mean when we use the term "ethical supply chain"? Implementing ethics in a supply chain generally means that we focus on increased corporate social responsibility, and that we are working on producing products and services while treating workers and the environment in an ethical way (Goldman n.d.). Therefore, supporting an ethical supply chain means that companies will incorporate social and human rights and environmental considerations into the way they are doing business across the world (Goldman n.d.).

Moreover, implementing an ethical supply chain need the right leadership skills that will not only allow the transformation to take place but also will facilitate the ethical transition and coherence between the supply chain actors. Therefore, leadership styles, for example, transformational leadership, can be essential for both proactive and reactive supply chain resilience, especially when combined with ambidextrous business models (Feng et al. 2024).

In general, it can be argued that the right supply chain governance, which can be expressed via the right leadership style as we saw in the previous paragraph, is extremely important in the modern business world as it can be able to address important environmental, social, and ethical impacts (Venkatarman et al. 2024).

Ethical supply chain governance can establish and administer ethical policies and sustainable/ethical practices (from procurement to customer service), while its effectiveness can support business operations through increased transparency, sustainability, and responsibility, which constitute an overall framework that can navigate decision-making supply chain-wise, mitigate risks and enhances the overall supply chain resilience (Venkatarman et al. 2024). In general, such governance and approach can literally contribute toward a more sustainable and ethically responsible business landscape (Venkatarman et al. 2024).

As a result, supply chain resilience can be enhanced via the implementation of an ethical business culture throughout the supply chain, a culture that need to have in its epicenter, humans, the environment, trust and respect among supply chain actors and need to be implemented by the right leadership.

Furthermore, ethical supply chains can foster collaboration and transparency between the various supply chain actors. This is extremely important as it ensures better communication and coordination, values that lead to improved supply chain resilience, since when unexpected disruptions occur, organizations with an ethical supply chain are better equipped to respond and maintain continuity of their supply chain (ethicalmarketer.org n.d.) via collaboration schemes that are based on mutual respect between the various supply chain actors.

In general, we can say that if companies, instead of adapting an ethical business model that will have people and planet in its epicenter and not just profit, apply a business model that will be based on underpaid workers, weak regulations, poor enforcement of labor laws, or even illegal activities, such as slavery or child labor, they will be unsustainable over a period of time (KPMG 2021), and when a crisis arises, they won't be able to be based on their people's effort to turn around the situation and help the company in question. Therefore, such companies will have a less resilient supply chain.

On the antipodes, a future-fit supply chain is the one that will be sustainable, collaborative, transparent, efficient, and agile (KPMG 2021). Such supply chain, which will be based on ethos and mutual trust and respect between supply chain actors, will be a very resilient since during a crisis all people involved will go the extra mile to help the supply chain to overcome the crisis and return to its previous status.

To be able to respond to change and/or disruptions successfully in its supply chain and to recover quickly, a company need to have an ethical supply chain, which will be based on an ethical business model that will take under consideration not only profit but also people and planet as interconnected elements of its triple bottom line.

Finally, we need to add that failing to integrate ethos along the supply chain is something that can expose it to various risks, such as loss of reputation, corruption, and social and environmental damages, which can give a hard blow to its resilience (as they will be preventive factors from let the company to operate in the way that it should during crisis in order to return to its previous situation as quickly as possible). Failing to integrate ethics along the supply chain leaves the door open to various risks, such as loss of reputation, corruption, and social and environmental damages that challenge supply chain resilience (Fritz 2022).

Use of Resilient Container Ports

Resilient supply chains need to be based on resilient infrastructure and mechanisms that can enhance their overall resilience. One of such infrastructures that we will discuss about in this subchapter is the container port, which is one of the main gateways for shipments in international and domestic trade logistics.

Container logistics supply chains are more service-oriented supply chains, which have container logistics as its core, while they try to integrate both upstream and downstream service providers and customers, and try to enhance service functions and to smooth operations (Xu et al. 2023). Since container logistics can handle large volumes of goods with low costs, they have become a serious component of today's international trade system (Xu et al. 2023).

Therefore, the stable and efficient operations of container logistics supply chains can enhance supply chain resilience via the strengthening of competences, which are related to responsibilities, rights, and interests of container ports, shipping companies, customers, and other related supply chain actors (Xu et al. 2023).

The core idea behind this strategy is that a resilient container port strategy can enhance the overall resilience of the supply chain in question. But building resilient container ports is something that requires reliable and consistent data, which will help supply chain professionals via the use of the right metrics to understand and target specific improvement areas and will assist them toward informed decision making that accordingly can boost the overall efficiency and resilience of the supply chain (Humphreys 2024).

Toward that direction, the World Bank and the S&P Global Market Intelligence have published the so-called "Container Port Performance Index," which has as its goal, via measuring and ranking the performance of more than 400 global ports to assist supply chain stakeholders to identify strengths (e.g., drive digital transformation), weaknesses (e.g., performance gaps), and opportunities (e.g., support investment decisions, foster collaboration, and policy development) for improvement toward the enhancement of the supply chain's efficiency and resilience (Humphreys 2024).

Resilient port containers to be able to improve the overall supply chain resilience need to follow specific strategies when implemented. Such strategies will not enhance their resilient during crisis, but also will fortify the resilience of the whole supply chain in question.

Therefore, they need to invest in port facilities in a way that they not only will be able to handle increased shipping volumes but also to support smoother, faster operations (Humphreys 2024). Of course, they need to be agile enough to adapt to circumstances since different disasters might have different characteristics, so such investments need to make port facilities ready to adapt to different circumstances. For example, during the financial crisis of 2008, shipping lines could not effectively manage their collective capacity, something that resulted in poor vessel utilization levels and even bailouts, while during the COVID-19 pandemic, shipping lines saw an upsurge of freight rates (Notteboom et al. 2021). Both examples indicate that different disruptions might have different effects to supply chain-related companies and can affect the operations of port facilities accordingly (e.g., increased number of containers, etc.), something that means that the investments in port facilities need, for example, to take place in a way that ports will be able to accommodate both occasions and so on.

Another strategy toward the same direction can be the adaption of advanced digital technologies in order to be able to streamline operations, reduce bureaucracy, and increase efficiency and speed in terms of data exchange, elements that will enhance overall operational efficiency, something that will positively impact the overall supply chain resilience as it will guarantee speed and efficiency for the whole supply chain during crisis, a paragon that can assist supply chains to rebound quickly (Humphreys 2024).

Another strategy is the building of connections between the ports and inland transportation networks, like railways, roads, and waterways, where possible, something that during crisis will ensure the seamless movement of goods from ports to their end destination, which will help supply chains to recover quickly (Humphreys 2024).

As we saw with the example of the two major recent crisis that supply chains experienced, ports are closely connected to how shipping lines are affected from the crisis. Therefore, establishing a close collaboration with stakeholders like shipping lines will assist ports during crisis to maintain continuity of operations and therefore better manage disruptions, something that will assist the whole supply chain to better rebound from crisis, thus to have increased resilience (Humphreys 2024).

Dual/ Multi Sourcing

As we presented till now in this chapter, enhancing supply chain resilience is a fundamental point that companies strive to achieve (Lou et al. 2024) via a diverse array of strategies, which can combine many elements of supply chain management, sustainability, and operations.

Since unforeseen factors like adverse weather, material shortages, recalls, natural disasters, and geopolitical issues can cause severe supply chain disruptions, which can heavily test supply chain resilience, supply chain professionals strive to find suitable strategies to adapt in order to increase both the robustness and the resilience of their supply chains. One of these strategies is the "dual sourcing" one (Gep.com 2023).

With the term dual sourcing, we mean a supply chain management strategy that involves engaging two suppliers to provide the company in question a specific component, material product, or a specific service, while it is interchangeably often used with "multisourcing," which is the case of involving more than two suppliers/sources (Gep. Com 2023).

The dual-sourcing strategy can enhance supply chain resilience as its implementation can minimize risk, as it reduces dependency on only one source; it can help supply chain professionals to address potential and unforeseen geopolitical challenges, accommodate capacity needs, and shorten lead times (Gep.com, 2023), as during a crisis, supply chain managers can turn to the second supplier if the first one cannot function or facing severe problems. In that way, production and sales can continue uninterrupted and easily rebound from the disruption that hit the first supplier.

What needs to be underlined, though, is that in order for such strategy to be successful, it needs a careful supplier selection, vulnerability identification, transparent communication, which will enhance trust and collaboration, and leveraging technology for, for example, real-time visibility enhancement (Gep.com 2023).

Dual-sourcing models have been adapted from many supply chain professionals throughout the world. The core idea behind such models is that they need to consider various SCR and risk attitudes and uncertain situations, while they try to develop a differentiated dual source procurement strategy to ensure supply chain stability and enhance supply chain resilience (Han et al. 2023).

Sometimes, the two sources that are involved in a dual-sourcing strategy might be one local and one overseas. When the situation is like that, different scenarios need to be taken under consideration, for example, a supply chain disruption at the overseas source may cause increased problems for the local supply chain than for the supply chain overseas from where the problem started (Zhu 2015). In addition, a significant cost saving can be achieved via the disruption in information if in such cases a firm orders from both sources, although information about the local source might be proved more valuable in some instances (Zhu 2015).

Collaboration is key in dual sourcing and in supply chain resilience, as we have already presented in this chapter. Therefore, collaboration under the prism of enhanced supply chain resilience is a critical dual-sourcing component, especially when a joint contract can be involved (Zhou et al. 2021). The reason behind this is that with a dual-sourcing strategy, which is cemented with a joint contract, a long-term supplier development strategy enhanced by a long-term technology cooperation can be established (Zhou et al. 2021). Such factors, as we have already discussed in this chapter, are critical for the strengthening of a supply chain's resilience.

Although dual sourcing can create some issues regarding costs and collaborations, its main strength lies in enhancing supply chain resilience (Gep.com 2023).

If companies embrace the dual-sourcing strategy, they can create adaptable networks capable of overcoming different challenges, while the "ripple effects" of this increased resilience in the supply chain can expand in the entire business ecosystem, by protecting operations, increasing customer satisfaction, and expanding market share (Gep.com 2023).

Therefore, implementing a dual- or even multisourcing strategy can be a catalyst toward an enhanced supply chain resilience as it can protect supply chains from several problem categories, including factors that can heavily test supply chain resilience like the ripple effect that we discussed in Chapter 2 and so on.

Supply Chain Innovation

There are several definitions of innovations. For example, according to *Cambridge Dictionary*, innovation is the use of a new idea or method, while the *American Heritage Dictionary* defines innovation as an act of introducing something new and so on (MIT Center for Transportation and Logistics 2012).

In the same wavelength, supply chain innovation is also hard to define. Bello et al. (2004, cited in MIT Center for Transportation and Logistics 2012) defined supply chain innovations as practices that combine developments in information and other related technologies with new logistics and marketing procedures toward the improvement of the operational efficiency and the effectiveness of services of a given supply chain.

It is also interesting to know that supply chain innovation at the process level, the last 20 years can be also found under the terms "change management" (Voropajev 1998, cited in MIT Center for Transportation and Logistics 2012), or "business process reengineering"

(Hammer 1990, cited in MIT Center for Transportation and Logistics 2012), or "continuous improvement" (Upton 1996, cited in MIT Center for Transportation and Logistics 2012), or "Kaizen" (Imai 1986, cited in MIT Center of Transportation and Logistics 2012).

Supply chain innovation plays an important role to the operational management practices as it can be seen the main factor behind the development of novel products and/or services, while it usually involves the use of new technologies (Malacina and Teplov 2022). Therefore, it can be said that supply chain innovation is a crucial paragon toward the enhancement of supply chain performance, sustainability and the acquisition of competitive advantage for a given supply chain (Malacina and Teplov 2022).

As we discussed in this chapter, supply chain resilience can be increased via the implementation of sustainability strategies, while another driver toward that direction can be the use of new technologies, which can increase efficiency, effectiveness, and supply chain visibility. Therefore, we can understand that the role that supply chain innovation can play toward an increased supply chain resilience is extremely important, as innovative supply chains can find new ways to tackle potential disruptions, especially via the use of new technologies as we have already discussed in this chapter.

The use of innovation toward enhancing supply chain resilience is highlighted by the following example. The example refers to a real-life case that deals with a medical device company, which invests in actionable visibility (Schuster et al. 2021). The example is about a global medical device manufacturer that had to meet a massive increase in demand during the COVID-19 pandemic. The company to maximize its throughput from its assembly lines focused on improving its supply chain management (Schuster et al. 2021).

The company in question quickly managed to establish a digital tool that translated production plans into sourcing requirements for parts, while it asked its tier-one suppliers to provide SKU-level weekly production plans for the four months to come and then input that data into its digital tool (Schuster et al. 2021). The idea was that by being able to match suppliers' production plans against the sourcing requirements, the manufacturer can pinpoint which critical parts might be the ones that probably are responsible for constraining production (Schuster et al. 2021). Then, after pinpointing these parts, the manufacturer collaborated with the suppliers of that parts in order to be able to maximize the parts' availability (Schuster et al. 2021).

Apart from the above, the company also set up a similar tool that gave it visibility into tier-two suppliers' availability in terms of products, while monitoring tier-one suppliers' ability to remove potential constraints that appeared in its assembly plans (Schuster et al. 2021).

The company also went one step further by creating a linear program that helped it to optimize the allocation of constrained materials across product models based on the two main factors, namely, the profitability and the strategic importance of customer orders (Schuster et al. 2021).

As a next step, the company consolidated the data that the new tools collected into the company's existing data in a way that it enabled informed decision making (Schuster et al. 2021). Such innovative solutions gave the company the opportunity to increase its volume output by 600 percent in only eight weeks' time (Schuster et al. 2021).

As we can see, increased visibility and increased performance, which are paragons of increased supply chain resilience have been achieved via the implementation of innovative digital solutions by the company.

Supply chains, especially nowadays, need to be dynamic and to keep pace with an ever-changing globalized world (Yu et al. 2019, cited in Ndonye and Wilson 2022), while they need to follow the new technologies. This dynamism that supply chains need to show today, is strongly connected with an increased supply chain resilience (Yu et al. 2019, cited in Ndonye and Wilson 2022). In other words, supply chains need to be dynamic to enhance their resilience.

While a supply chain being dynamic has to do with its capacity to purposefully create, extend, or modify the base of its resources (Helfat 2007, cited in Wang et al. 2020, 85, cited in Ndonye and Wilson 2022), innovation can be considered as one of the main dynamic capabilities that a dynamic supply chain needs to have in order to be able to increase its resilience (Kamalahmadi and Parast 2016, cited in Ndonye and Wilson 2022). This is why, the acceleration of innovation in companies is consider by many as one of the most important objectives of the fourth industrial revolution (Frank et al. 2019, cited in Wnag et al. 2020, 84, cited in Ndonye and Wilson 2022).

The role that supply chain innovation plays in an increased supply chain resilience is evident. A supply chain, which has established innovation strategies, would be a more resilient one, simply because innovation can assist companies toward strengthening their capabilities that positively affect risk management and therefore, supply chain resilience (Sabahi and Mahour 2020). Supply chain innovation can support capabilities like knowledge sharing, agility, flexibility, which accordingly can enhance supply chain resilience (Sabahi and Mahour 2020).

Overall, companies that want to enhance their supply chain resilience might need to embed a culture of innovation in their supply chains, which will be aligned with the overall supply chain strategy. Then, and always via the prism of dynamic supply chains, supply chain resilience can be enhanced due to the increase of collaboration, agility, knowledge sharing, and the use of new technologies.

Several innovations can be used today toward enhancing supply chain resilience. Most of them are connected to new technologies that came with the advent of Industries 4.0 and 5.0. Some have already been discussed in the technology part of this chapter.

An important element of contemporary supply chains that can make a difference is data collection. Today, data collection has been enhanced via the use of IoT technologies and has been used to help supply chain professionals to predict spikes in demand and to pinpoint, if possible, supply chain and/or market disruptions toward a quick reaction and/or quick recovery (Iftikhar et al. 2024). Therefore, one can argue that the implementation of IoT-enabled innovative technologies has helped companies in terms of navigating through the difficult landscape of supply chain disruptions and enhancing their supply chain resilience (Iftikhar et al. 2024).

Digital innovation should be in the forefront of contemporary supply chains as it can increase their resilience and help them acquire

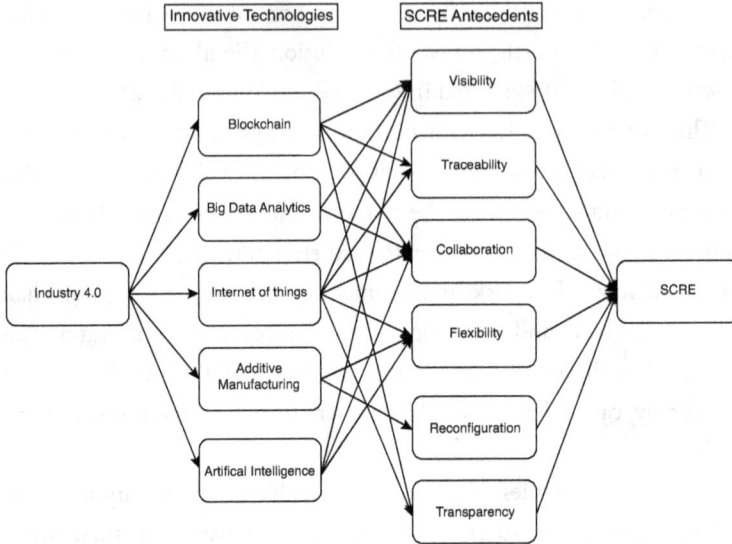

Figure 3.1 *Innovative technologies and supply chain resilience (Iftikhar et al. 2024)*

their competitive advantage (Gelende et al. 2020; Martin 2020, cited in Iftikhar et al. 2024).

In addition to the above, the use of supply chain data analytics systems and especially big data analytics will be a game changer for supply chain professionals (Iftikhar et al. 2024). Their contribution in enhanced forecasting can assist companies not only in predicting potential future disruptions, but also to enhance their supply chain resilience as they will be able to proactively take precaution measures that will assist them to rebound more quickly when disruptions will occur.

Similarly, Kadadevavaramth et al. (2020, cited in Iftikhar et al. 2024) mentioned that the use of IoT-enabled technologies like data analytics can enhance supply chain resilience by providing access to real-time data via the use of information sharing, collaboration, and preprogrammed responses.

In Figure 3.1, we can see how the use of innovative new technologies can enhance supply chain resilience via their positive influence on supply chain antecedents like visibility, traceability, collaboration, flexibility, reconfiguration, and transparency.

An example on how the use of advanced data analytics can improve supply chain resilience comes from Canada, where the Canadian fertilizer company Nutrient, which operates around 24 manufacturing and processing facilities all over the world and nearly 2,000 retail stores in the United States and Australia, uses of a combination of cloud technology and AI/machine learning capabilities to collect underutilized data in order to be able to increase its supply chain visibility and enhance its supply chain resilience (technologyreview.com 2024).

The advent of Industry 4.0 brought a technological revolution, which was represented with IoT-enabled innovations like the ones that we discussed in the previous paragraphs. The decedent of Industries 4.0 and 5.0, brought with it far more advanced systems and technologies, which via their breakthrough innovation[**] nature is already in position to influence supply chains and especially supply chain resilience.

Of course, one problem at this time might be the higher cost that such disruptive innovations, which makes it important for companies that want to implement it to implement first a benefit-cost analysis in order to determine whether or not this is something that is feasible for them in the present time.

Such innovations, for example, the use of autonomous robots in supply chains, can redefine them and can help companies to increase supply chain resilience via the enhancement of efficiency, flexibility, and effectiveness in their supply chains, as autonomous robots can assist companies to decrease long-term costs, provide labor and utilization stability, increase worker productivity, reduce error rate, reduce frequency of inventory checks, optimize picking/sorting and sorting times, and increase access to dangerous locations (Deloitte.com 2024).

[**] Break through innovation: "It's a type of innovation, that is not merely about incremental advancements; rather, it's a leap into the uncharted territory of novel ideas, redefining industries and reshaping customer experiences. In the words of the entrepreneur, breakthrough innovation is the key to unlocking unprecedented value" (digitalleadership.com 2023).

Notes for the Teacher

In this chapter, we presented several/the most important and well-used strategies that companies can implement in their supply chains to make them more resilient.

Discussion Points

1. A discussion about each one of the strategies and/or their potential combination could be take place in the classroom.
2. Another discussion might be how each strategy can be used in order to address each one of the factors that were presented in Chapter 2, and which can affect the resilience of the supply chain.
   a. Can more than one strategy be applied to mitigate these factors?
   b. How complex and/or doable is for a company to implement a combination of the presented strategies?
3. Discuss about the potential cost of each one of the strategies, the resources needed, how such strategies can be combined with the overall company strategy, which might be the consequences for other parts of the company's operations, like customer service, production, logistics, and so on.
4. Give examples with companies that implemented one or more of the presented strategies.
   a. How did they do that?
   b. Did that assist them to acquire a competitive advantage in their respective industry?
5. As a conclusive discussion, you can discuss with the students the importance of supply chain resilience as seen under the prism of the triple bottom line. You can extrapolate the results of the discussion on today's reality with real-life examples of resilient supply chains and factors that heavily test their resilience (natural or unnatural ones). You can conclude the discussion by mentioning the importance of an ethical supply chain and

explaining why this is extremely important from a societal point of view with examples like medicine logistics during the crisis and so on.

Epilogue

In a world that is changing so fast and amidst the advent of Industry 5.0, supply chain professionals have started to understand the importance of a robust and resilient supply chain. In this book, we focused on supply chain resilience, and we investigated it by following two distinct steps. First, we tried to understand which are the paragons that can impose some pressure on supply chain resilience, while as a second step, we proposed some strategies that supply chain professionals would be nice to follow to increase the resilience of their supply chains.

Global disruptions today have many faces as we have several recent examples toward that direction, like the COVID-19 pandemic, the Suez Canal blockage, the Ukraine and the Gaza wars, and several natural disasters, like tsunamis and so on. Such unforeseen events not only disrupt global supply chains but also create vast societal problems, which are very difficult to address, especially when, for example, logistics are not able to deliver medicines and/or support people who are devastated by natural or unnatural disasters and so on.

Supply chain professionals, governments, and organizations, and eventually, all stakeholders who are involved one way or another in supply chain management need to take some action to increase supply chain resilience no matter the industry in which they operate.

Therefore, the importance of this book is huge as it deals, in a concise and reader-friendly way, with a very contemporary issue, which can have severe global implications.

The different strategies that are suggested by this book are not exhaustive, but instead, indicative, and are presented in a way that can give directions to supply chain professionals toward sustainable and resilient solutions. Potential combinations of different strategies can enhance supply chain resilience even more and can strengthen and make more efficient all supply chain operations.

Epilogue

A Message From the Author

No matter which strategy each supply chain professional chooses and no matter the potential combination between them, what is of the utmost importance is that such a strategy needs to be combined with ethos.

Creating ethical supply chains not only strengthens supply chain resilience but also increases transparency, information flow, and collaboration between all supply chain stakeholders from all over the world. This ethical dimension per se underlines the positive social implications that ethical supply chains can have. In turbulent times, and during natural disasters or pandemics, having an ethical base upon which to build your supply chain is something that is extremely important and can have vast positive societal implications.

The "people" aspect of the triple bottom line is extremely important, especially today, as the challenges grow, although many supply chain actors have not yet realized the importance of embedding ethos in their supply chains. Ethical supply chains can make a huge difference, they can be resilient and robust and can change the world towards a better future.

References

Abe, Masato and Linghe Ye. 2013. "Building Resilient Supply Chains Against Natural Disasters: The Cases of Japan and Thailand." *Global Business Review* 14 (4): 567-586.

Ali, A.A.A, A.A.A Sharabati, M. Allahham, and A.Y. Nasereddin. 2024. "The Relationship Between Supply Chain Resilience and Digital Supply Chain and the Impact on Sustainability: Supply Chain Dynamism as a Moderator." *Sustainability* 16 (7): 3082.

Althaf, S. and C.W. Babbitt. 2021. "Disruption Risks to Material Supply Chains in the Electronics Sector." *Resources, Conservation and Recycling* 167: 105248.

Alfarsi, F., F. Lemke, and Y. Yang. 2019. "The Importance of Supply Chain Resilience: An Empirical Investigation." *Procedia Manufacturing* 39: 1525–1529.

Al Naimi, M., M.N. Faisal, R. Sobh, and S.M.F. Uddin. 2021. "Antecedents and Consequences of Supply Chain Resilience and Reconfiguration: An Empirical Study in an Emerging Economy." *Journal of Enterprise Information Management* 34 (6): 1722–1745.

Alexander, D.L., J.A. Al-Khatib, M.I. Al-Habib, N. Bogari, and N. Salamah. 2019. "Business Culture's Influence on Negotiators' Ethical Ideologies and Judgment: An Eight-Country Study." *Journal of Marketing Theory and Practice* 27 (3): 312–330.

Ambrogio, G., L. Filice, F. Longo, and A. Padovano. 2022. "Workforce and Supply Chain Disruption as a Digital and Technological Innovation Opportunity for Resilient Manufacturing Systems in the COVID-19 Pandemic." *Computers & Industrial Engineering* 169: 108158–108158.

Amico, Ambra, Luca Verginer, Giona Casiraghi, Giacomo Vaccario, and Frank Schweitzer. 2023. "Adapting to Disruptions: Flexibility as a Pillar of Supply Chain Resilience." *ArXiv* (Cornell University).

Aming'a, Mary, Reuben Marwanga, and Jonathan Annan. 2024. "Is it Practical to Uphold Both Resilience and Sustainability of Supply Chains Using Closed-Loop Supply Chain Models Considering Circular Economy? an Empirical Investigation From Kenya." *Cogent Business & Management* 11 (1).

Ancarani, Alessandro, Carmela Di Mauro, and Francesco Mascali. 2019. "Backshoring Strategy and the Adoption of Industry 4.0: Evidence From Europe." *Journal of World Business : JWB* 54 (4): 360–371.

Arvis, Jean-Francois, Jean-Francois Marteau, and Gael Raballand. 2010. *The Cost of Being Landlocked: Logistics Costs and Supply Chain Reliability*, 1st ed. Herndon: World Bank. doi:10.1596/978-0-8213-8408-4.

Aslam, Haris, Abdul Qadeer Khan, Kamran Rashid, and Saif-ur Rehman. 2020. "Achieving Supply Chain Resilience: The Role of Supply Chain Ambidexterity and Supply Chain Agility." *Journal of Manufacturing Technology Management* 31(6): 1185-1204.

ASCM.org, 2020. Close the Supply Chain Skills Gap with Reskilling and Upskilling [Online]. Available at:< Close the Supply Chain Skills Gap with Reskilling and Upskilling (ascm.org)> [Accessed 8 August 2024].

Baah, Charles, Douglas Opoku Agyeman, Innocent Senyo Kwasi Acquah, Yaw Agyabeng-Mensah, Ebenezer Afum, Kassimu Issau, Daniel Ofori, and Daniel Faibil. 2022. "Effect of Information Sharing in Supply Chains: Understanding the Roles of Supply Chain Visibility, Agility, Collaboration on Supply Chain Performance." *Benchmarking : An International Journal* 29 (2): 434–455.

Badwan, Nemer. 2024. "Role of Supply Chain Partnership, Cross-Functional Integration, Responsiveness and Resilience on competitive Advantages: Empirical Evidence from Palestine." *TQM Journal.*

Bahrami, Mohamad and Sajjad Shokouhyar. 2022. "The Role of Big Data Analytics Capabilities in Bolstering Supply Chain Resilience and Firm Performance: A Dynamic Capability View." *Information Technology & People (West Linn, Or.)* 35 (5): 1621–1651.

Basnet, Chuda. 2013. "The Measurement of Internal Supply Chain Integration." *Management Research Review* 36 (2): 153–172.

Behzadi, G., M.J. O'Sullivan, and T.L. Olsen. 2020. "On Metrics for Supply Chain Resilience." *European Journal of Operational Research* 287(1): 145–158.

Behzadi, Golnar, Michael Justin O'Sullivan, and Tava Lennon Olsen. 2020. "On Metrics for Supply Chain Resilience." *European Journal of Operational Research* 287 (1): 145–158.

Bhattacharjee D., Bustamante F., Curley A., Perez F., 2021. "Navigating the Labor Mismatch in US Logistics and Supply Chains." McKinsey and Company. Accessed June 16, 2024.

Brandon-Jones, Emma, Brian Squire, Chad W. Autry, and Kenneth J. Petersen. 2014. "A Contingent Resource-Based Perspective of Supply Chain Resilience and Robustness." *The Journal of Supply Chain Management* 50 (3): 55–73.

Britt H., 2021. "What Is Upstream and Downstream in Supply Chain Management." Thomasnet.com. Accessed August 28, 2024. www.thomasnet.com/insights/what-is-upstream-downstream-supply-chain-management/?msockid=2dd872278e71642d03a3664c8f79654d.

Bø, Eirill, Inger Beate Hovi, and Daniel Ruben Pinchasik. 2023. "COVID-19 Disruptions and Norwegian Food and Pharmaceutical Supply Chains: Insights Into Supply Chain Risk Management, Resilience, and Reliability." *Sustainable Futures* 5: 100102–100102.

Buchholz L., 2023. Unlocking the Power of a Diverse and Inclusive Supply Chain. Sustainabilitymag.com. Accessed August 27, 2024. https://sustainabilitymag. com/articles/unlocking-the-power-of-a-diverse-and-inclusive-supply-chain.

Byrne R.O. 2020. "7 Mini Case Studies: Successful Supply Chain Cost-Reduction and Management." Trans.info. Accessed August 29, 2024. https:// trans.info/en/7-mini-case-studies-successful-supply-chain-cost-reduction-and-management-174252.

Carissimi, Maria Concetta, Alessandro Creazza, and Claudia Colicchia. 2023. "Crossing the Chasm: Investigating the Relationship between Sustainability and Resilience in Supply Chain Management." *Cleaner Logistics and Supply Chain* 7: 100098.

Cambridge.dictionary.org., n.d. "Upskilling, Reskilling." Accessed August 27, 2024. https://dictionary.cambridge.org/dictionary/english/reskilling.

Chen, Ping-Kuo, Yong Ye, and Xiang Huang. 2023a. "The Metaverse in Supply Chain Knowledge Sharing and Resilience Contexts: An Empirical Investigation of Factors Affecting Adoption and Acceptance." *Journal of Innovation & Knowledge* 8(4): 100446.

Chen, Guangxin, Qing Nie, and Hui Zhao. 2023b. "The Influence Factors of Organizational Resilience From a CSR Perspective and Their Impact on Business Growth." *Sustainability* 15(22): 15712.

Chod, Jiri, Nikolaos Trichakis, and Gerry Tsoukalas. 2019. "Supplier Diversification Under Buyer Risk." *Management Science* 65 (7): 3150–3173.

Cohen, Morris, Shiliang Cui, Sebastian Doetsch, Ricardo Ernst, Arnd Huchzermeier, Panos Kouvelis, Hau Lee, Hirofumi Matsuo, and Andy A. Tsay. 2022. "Bespoke Supply-Chain Resilience: The Gap Between Theory and Practice." *Journal of Operations Management* 68 (5): 515–531.

Columbia.edu., n.d. "Hold -up Problem. Accessed August 29, 2024. www. columbia.edu/~yc2271/files/papers/holdup.pdf.

Cority.com. 2023. "Diversity, Equity & Inclusion (DE&I) in Supply Chains." Assessed August 8, 2024www.cority.com/blog/diversity-equity-inclusion-dei-in-supply-chains/.

Cotta, Diogo, Lester Klink, Thorsten Alten, and Belal Al Madhoon. 2023. "How Do Supply Chain Managers Perceive the Relationship Between Resilience and Sustainability Practices? An Exploratory Study." *Business Strategy and the Environment* 32(6): 3737–3751.

Dau.edu. n.d. "Critical Component. Accessed August 13, 2024.

Deloitte, n.d. "Supply Chain Management and Modernization in Government." Accessed April 20, 2023. www2.deloitte.com/us/en/pages/public-sector/ solutions/supply-chain-management-government.html?id=us:2ps: 3bi:gpsvasc22:awa:gps:010923:supply%20chain%20resiliency:p:c :kwd-77584560167379:loc-129&msclkid=a738e6485fd41ae6354a82094f0 d838d.

Delloitte.com, 2024. "Using Autonomous Robots to Drive Supply Chain Innovation. Accessed August 27, 2024. www2.deloitte.com/us/en/pages/manufacturing/articles/autonomous-robots-supply-chain-innovation.html.

Dennehy, Denis, John Oredo, Konstantina Spanaki, Stella Despoudi, and Mike Fitzgibbon. 2021. "Supply Chain Resilience in Mindful Humanitarian Aid Organizations: The Role of Big Data Analytics." *International Journal of Operations & Production Management* 41(9): 1417–1441.

Dictionary.cambridge.org, n.d. "Supply Chain Resilience." Accessed November 13, 2022. https://dictionary.cambridge.org/dictionary/english/resilience.

Digitalleadership.com. 2023. "Breakthrough Innovation Examples, Definition, and How to Create." Accessed August 27, 2024. https://digitalleadership.com/glossary/breakthrough-innovation-definition/.

Diodato, Dario, Franco Malerba, and Andrea Morrison. 2018. "The Made-in Effect and Leapfrogging: A Model of Leadership Change for Products With Country-of-Origin Bias." *European Economic Review* 101: 297–329.

Dolgui, Alexandre and Dmitry Ivanov. 2021. "Ripple Effect and Supply Chain Disruption Management: New Trends and Research Directions." *International Journal of Production Research* 59 (1): 102–109.

Dolgui, Alexandre, Dmitry Ivanov, and Boris Sokolov. 2018. "Ripple Effect in the Supply Chain: An Analysis and Recent Literature." *International Journal of Production Research* 56(1–2): 414–430.

Dolgui, Alexandre, Dmitry Ivanov, and Maxim Rozhkov. 2020. "Does the Ripple Effect Influence the Bullwhip Effect? An Integrated Analysis of Structural and Operational Dynamics in the Supply Chain." *International Journal of Production Research* 58(5): 1285–1301.

Dubey, Rameshwar, David J. Bryde, Yogesh K. Dwivedi, Gary Graham, Cyril Foropon, and Thanos Papadopoulos. 2023. "Dynamic Digital Capabilities and Supply Chain Resilience: The Role of Government Effectiveness." *International Journal of Production Economics* 258: 108790.

Dyatkin, Boris. 2020. "COVID-19 Pandemic Highlights Need for US Policies that Increase Supply Chain Resilience." *MRS Bulletin* 45(10): 794–796.

Ecb.europa.eu. 2021. "What Is Driving the Recent Urge in Shipping Costs?" Accessed August 9, 2024. www.ecb.europa.eu/press/economic-bulletin/focus/2021/html/ecb.ebbox202103_01~8ecbf2b17c.en.html.

Edeh F.O., Ugboego A.C., Adama L., 2020. "Human Resource Skills Adjustment and Organisational Resilience in Times of Global Crisis." *Kelaniya Journal of Human Resource Management* 17: 1. https://kjhrm.sljol.info/articles/10.4038/kjhrm.v17i1.70.

Edureka.co. 2022. "What Is A Supply Chain Control Tower? Types & Uses." Accessed August 29, 2024. www.edureka.co/blog/supply-chain-control-tower/.

El Baz, Jamal and Salomée Ruel. 2021. "Can Supply Chain Risk Management Practices Mitigate the Disruption Impacts on Supply Chains' Resilience and

Robustness? Evidence from an Empirical Survey in a COVID-19 Outbreak Era." *International Journal of Production Economics* 233: 107972–107972.

El Korchi, Akram. 2022. "Survivability, Resilience and Sustainability of Supply Chains: The COVID-19 Pandemic." *Journal of Cleaner Production* 377: 134363–134363.

Eskhenazi A. 2021. "Supply Chains Encounter a Global Raw Materials Crisis." Assessed April 20, 2023. www.ascm.org/ascm-insights/scm-now-impact/supply-chains-encounter-a-global-raw-materials-crisis/.

Ethicalmarketer.org. n.d. "Ethical Supply Chain Creating a Sustainable and Responsible Business." Accessed August 27, 2024. https://ethicalmarketer.org/ethical-supply-chain-creating-sustainable-and-responsible-business/.

Eversheds-sutherland.com. 2024. "International Trade and Sanctions: How Global Trade Regulation is Reshaping Supply Chains." Accessed August 28, 2024. www.eversheds-sutherland.com/en/global/insights/how-global-trade-regulation-is-reshaping-supply-chains.

Feng, Taiwen, Zhihui Si, Wenbo Jiang, and Jianyu Tan. 2024. "Supply Chain Transformational Leadership and Resilience: The Mediating Role of Ambidextrous Business Model." *Humanities & Social Sciences Communications* 11(1): 628–12.

Faruquee, Murtaza, Antony Paulraj, and Chandra Ade Irawan. 2021. "Strategic Supplier Relationships and Supply Chain Resilience: Is Digital Transformation That Precludes Trust Beneficial?" *International Journal of Operations & Production Management* 41(7): 1192–1219.

Fema.org. n.d. "Supply Chain Resilience Guide." Accessed August 11, 2024. www.fema.gov/sites/default/files/2020-07/supply-chain-resilience-guide.pdf.

Fernández-Miguel, Andrés, Maria Pia Riccardi, Valerio Veglio, Fernando E. García-Muiña, Alfonso P Fernández del Hoyo, and Davide Settembre-Blundo. 2022. "Disruption in Resource-Intensive Supply Chains: Reshoring and Nearshoring as Strategies to Enable Them to Become More Resilient and Sustainable." *Sustainability* 14(17): 10909.

Fiksel, Joseph. 2006. "Sustainability and Resilience: Toward a Systems Approach"." *Sustainability: Science, Practice & Policy* 2(2): 1–8.

Fiksel J., M. Polyviou, K.L. Croxton, and I. Pettit. 2014. "From Risk to Resilience: Learning to Deal With Disruption." Sloanreview.mit.edu. Accessed August 9, 2024. https://sloanreview.mit.edu/article/from-risk-to-resilience-learning-to-deal-with-disruption/.

Fritz, M.M.C. 2022. "Ethical Supply Chain Practices to Achieve Supply Chain Resilience." In *Yanamandra Ramakrisha, Handbook of Research on Supply Chain Resiliency, Efficiency and Visibility in the Post- pandemic Era*, 402–422. IGI Global. DOI: 10.4018/978-1-7998-9506-0. chain practices to achieve supply chain resilience. In: Yanamandra Ramakrishna, Handbook of Research on Supply Chain Resiliency, Efficiency, and Visibility in the Post-Pandemic Era. IGI Global, pp. 402–422. DOI: 10.4018/978-1-7998-9506-0.ch020

Fritz, M. M. C. (2022). Ethical supply chain practices to achieve supply chain resilience. In: Yanamandra Ramakrishna, Handbook of Research on Supply Chain Resiliency, Efficiency, and Visibility in the Post-Pandemic Era. IGI Global, pp. 402–422. DOI: 10.4018/978-1-7998-9506-0.ch02

Gep.com, 2021. Three definite characteristics of an agile and resilient supply chain [blog] Available at:< 3 Definitive Characteristics of an Agile & Resilient Supply Chain | GEP> [Assessed 20 December 2022].

Gep.com. 2023. "Dual Sourcing: A Safety Net During Supply Chain Disruptions." Accessed August 13, 2024. www.gep.com/blog/strategy/dual-sourcing-benefits-challenges-strategies#:~:text=Dual%20Sourcing%3A%20A%20Safety%20Net%20During%20Supply%20Chain,resilience%2C%20accommodating%20capacity%20needs%20and%20shortening%20lead%20times.Gep.com. n.d. "What Is Supply Chain Agility?." Accessed August 26, 2024. www.gep.com/knowledge-bank/glossary/what-is-supply-chain-agility.

Gerrit. n.d. Freightcourse.com. "A Guide to Break Bulk Terminals." Accessed August 29, 2024. www.freightcourse.com/break-bulk-terminals.

Ghadge, Abhijeet, Maximilian Weiß, Nigel D. Caldwell, and Richard Wilding. 2020. "Managing Cyber Risk in Supply Chains: A Review and Research Agenda." *Supply Chain Management* 25(2): 223–240.

Giannoccaro, Ilaria and Anas Iftikhar. 2022. "Mitigating Ripple Effect in Supply Networks: The Effect of Trust and Topology on Resilience." *International Journal of Production Research* 60(4): 1178–1195.

Goebel, Philipp, Carsten Reuter, Richard Pibernik, and Christina Sichtmann. 2012. "The Influence of Ethical Culture on Supplier Selection in the Context of Sustainable Sourcing." International Journal of Production Economics 140 (1): 7-17.

Goldman S. n.d. The-Future-of-Commerce.com. "The Ethical Supply Chain: Definition, Examples, Stats"." Accessed August 11, 2024. www.the-future-of-commerce.com/2020/01/22/ethical-supply-chain-definition-stats/.

Golnar B., Michael Justin O'Sullivan, and Tava Lennon Olsen. 2020. "On Metrics for Supply Chain Resilience." *European Journal of Operational Research* 287(1): 145–158.

Grappi, Silvia, Simona Romani, and Richard P. Bagozzi. 2020. "Consumer Reshoring Sentiment and Animosity: Expanding our Understanding of Market Responses to Reshoring." *Management International Review* 60(1): 69–95.

Gu, Minhao, Lu Yang, and Baofeng Huo. 2021;2020;. "The Impact of Information Technology Usage on Supply Chain Resilience and Performance: An Ambidextrous View." *International Journal of Production Economics* 232: 107956–107956.

Guillot C, 2018. "As Disruptions Accelerate, Supply Chains Learn to Measure Them." Accessed March 27, 2023. www.supplychaindive.com/news/disaster-planning-supply-chain-KPIs/542047/.

Gumusburun Ayalp, Gulden and Tülay Çivici. 2023. "Factors Affecting the Performance of Construction Industry during the COVID-19 Pandemic: A Case Study in Turkey." *Engineering, Construction, and Architectural Management* 30 (8): 3160–3202.

Han, Y., W.K. Chong, and D. Li. 2020."A Systematic Literature Review of the Capabilities and Performance Metrics of Supply Chain Resilience." *International Journal of Production Research* 58(15): 4541–4566.

Han, Neungho and Juneho Um. 2024. "Risk Management Strategy for Supply Chain Sustainability and Resilience Capability." *Risk Management* 26(2): 6.

Han, Bing, Ying Zhang, Song Wang, and Yongshin Park. 2023. "The Efficient and Stable Planning for Interrupted Supply Chain With Dual-Sourcing Strategy: A Robust Optimization Approach Considering Decision Maker's Risk Attitude." *Omega (Oxford)* 115: 102775.

Hanbury and Hoecker. 2021. Bain.com. "Two Lessons the Chip Shortage Taught Us About Supply Chains." Accessed August 13, 2024. www.bain.com/insights/two-lessons-from-the-chip-shortage-supply-chains-tech-report-2021/.

He, Juan, Chao Ma, and Kai Pan. 2017. "Capacity Investment in Supply Chain With Risk Averse Supplier Under Risk Diversification Contract." *Transportation Research. Part E, Logistics and Transportation Review* 106: 255–275.

Hida Syahchari, Dicky, Darjat Sudrajat, Lasmy Lasmy, Maria Grace Herlina, Fanny Estefania, and Erik Van Zanten. 2022. "Achieving Supply Chain Resilience Through Supply Chain Risk Management and Supply Chain Partnership."*ACM*. doi:10.1145/3512676.3512712.

Hines, Tony. 2012. *Supply Chain Strategies*. London: Routledge.

Hohenstein, Nils-Ole, Edda Feisel, Evi Hartmann, and Larry Giunipero. 2015. "Research on the Phenomenon of Supply Chain Resilience: A Systematic Review and Paths for further Investigation." *International Journal of Physical Distribution & Logistics Management* 45(1–2): 90–117.

Huang, Yung-Fu, Vu-Dung-Van Phan, and Manh-Hoang Do. 2023. "The Impacts of Supply Chain Capabilities, Visibility, Resilience on Supply Chain Performance and Firm Performance." *Administrative Sciences* 13(10): 225.

Huang, Xiang and Ping-Kuo Chen. 2022. "A Systematic Literature Review Exploring the Relationship Between Metaverse and Supply Chain Resilience: The Role of Sensory Feedback."*ACM*. doi:10.1145/3589860.3589872.

Humphreys R.M., 2024. Blogs.worldbank.org. "How Resilient Ports Can Mitigate Global Supply Chain Disruptions". Accessed August 11, 2024. https://blogs.worldbank.org/en/transport/how-resilient-ports-can-mitigate-global-supply-chain-disruptions.

IBM.com. n.d. "All Supply Chains Are Digital." Accessed August 10, 2024. www.ibm.com/thought-leadership/institute-business-value/en-us/report/supply-chain-cybersecurity.

Iftikhar, Anas, Laura Purvis, Ilaria Giannoccaro, and Yingli Wang. 2023. "The Impact of Supply Chain Complexities on Supply Chain Resilience: The Mediating Effect of Big Data Analytics." *Production Planning & Control* 34(16): 1562–1582.

Inboundlogistics.com. 2023. "Supply Chain Visibility: What It Is, Importance, and Types." Accessed August 26, 2024. www.inboundlogistics.com/articles/supply-chain-visibility/.

Intuendi.com. 2024. "Supply Chain Disruption: Causes, Effects, and Management." Accessed August 14, 2024. https://intuendi.com/resource-center/supply-chain-disruption/.

Ivanov, Dmitry. 2023. "Intelligent Digital Twin (iDT) for Supply Chain Stress-Testing, Resilience, and Viability." *International Journal of Production Economics* 263: 108938.

Jain, Nikunj Kumar, Kaustov Chakraborty, and Piyush Choudhary. 2024. "Building Supply Chain Resilience through Industry 4.0 Base Technologies: Role of Supply Chain Visibility and Environmental Dynamism." *The Journal of Business & Industrial Marketing* 39(8): 1750–1763.

Just Imagination Blog. 2022. "Supply Chain Resiliency: Three Companies With Resilient Supply Chains Setting the Example [blog]." Accessed March 27, 2023. https://blog.jcu.edu/2022/04/27/companies-with-supply-chain-resilience/.

Katsaliaki, K., P. Galetsi, and S. Kumar. 2022. "Supply Chain Disruptions and Resilience: A Major Review and Future Research Agenda." *Annals of Operations Research* 319(1): 965–1002.

Katsuki A., Lennerfors T., 2013. "Improved Keiretsu." "The New." Accessed August 5, 2024. https://hbr.org/2013/09/the-new-improved-keiretsu.

Kazancoglu, Yigit, Cisem Lafci, Yalcin Berberoglu, Arvind Upadhyay, Luis Rocha-Lona, and Vikas Kumar. 2024. "The Effects of Globalization on Supply Chain Resilience: Outsourcing Techniques as Interventionism, Protectionism, and Regionalization Strategies." *Operations Management Research* 17(2): 505–522.

Kirvan P. 2022. TechTarget. "Use Recovery Level Objective to Fine-Tune BCDR Response." Accessed March 27, 2023. www.techtarget.com/searchdisasterrecovery/tip/Use-recovery-level-objective-to-fine-tune-BCDR-response.

Kouvelis, Panos, bA Chen, and Yu Xia. 2023. "Managing Material Shortages in Project Supply Chains: Inventories, Time Buffers, and Supplier Flexibility." *Production and Operations Management* 32(11): 3717–3735.

KPMG. 2021. "Ethical Supply Chains and Procurement." Accessed August 27, 2024. https://assets.kpmg.com/content/dam/kpmg/xx/pdf/2021/07/ethical-supply-chains-and-procurement.pdf.

Kuehne -Nagel, n.d. Kuehne+Nagel. "From Just in Time to Just in Case." Accessed April 20, 2023. https://home.kuehne-nagel.com/en/-/services/supply-chain/supply-chain-management-4pl-logistics-resilience.

Larsen, 2024 Maersk. "5 Reasons to Implement Supply Chain Diversification." Accessed August 5, 2024. www.maersk.com/insights/resilience/2024/06/04/five-reasons-to-diversify-your-supply-chain.

Le, Thanh Tiep and Abhishek Behl. 2024. "Linking Artificial Intelligence and Supply Chain Resilience: Roles of Dynamic Capabilities Mediator and Open Innovation Moderator." *IEEE Transactions on Engineering Management* 71: 8577–8590.

Lean.org., n.d. "What is Lean?" Accessed August 26, 2024. www.lean.org/explore-lean/what-is-lean/.Lebovitz R., 2021. Future of Sourcing. "The Big Supply Chain Talent Shortage. Accessed June 16, 2024. https://futureofsourcing.com/the-big-supply-chain-talent-shortage/.

Lee, Voon Hsien, Pik-Yin Foo, Tat-Huei Cham, Teck-Soon Hew, Garry Wei-Han Tan, and Keng-Boon Ooi. 2024. "Big Data Analytics Capability in Building Supply Chain Resilience: The Moderating Effect of Innovation-Focused Complementary Assets." *Industrial Management + Data Systems* 124(3): 1203–1233.

Lee, Neil Chueh-An. 2021. "Reconciling Integration and Reconfiguration Management Approaches in the Supply Chain." *International Journal of Production Economics* 242: 108288.

Levis T. 2021. Supply & Demand Chain Executive (sdcexec.com). "Upskilling and Reskilling Workers to Improve Supply Chain Resilience." Accessed August 8, 2024. www.sdcexec.com/professional-development/training/article/21521017/ascentis-upskilling-and-reskilling-workers-to-improve-supply-chain-resilience.

Li, Wenjie and Elise Miller-Hooks. 2023. "Understanding the Implications of Port-Related Workforce Shortages on Global Maritime Performance through the Study of a Carrier Alliance." *Maritime Economics & Logistics* 25(3): 452–478.

Li, Lin, Zhaojun Yang, and Chrissie Diane Tan. 2019. ""Buffer Inventory + Information Sharing." Strategy for Retailers in Two-Level Fresh Supply Chain." *IEEE*. doi:10.1109/IEEM44572.2019.8978846.

Li, Ying, Jing Dai, and Li Cui. 2020. "The Impact of Digital Technologies on Economic and Environmental Performance in the Context of Industry 4.0: A Moderated Mediation Model." *International Journal of Production Economics* 229: 107777.

Lido.app. n.d. "Buffer Inventory. Everything You Need to Know in 2024." Accessed August 5, 2024.

Longo, Francesco, Giovanni Mirabelli, Antonio Padovano, and Vittorio Solina. 2023. "The Digital Supply Chain Twin Paradigm for Enhancing Resilience and Sustainability Against COVID-Like Crises." *Procedia Computer Science* 217: 1940–1947.

Lou, Gaoxiang, Yuhan Guo, Zhixuan Lai, Haicheng Ma, and Xuechen Tu. 2024. "Optimal Resilience Strategy for Manufacturers to Deal With Supply Disruptions: Investment in Supply Stability Versus Dual Sourcing." *Computers & Industrial Engineering* 190: 110030.

Lip G. n.d. Corporatefinanceinstitute.com. "Offshoring." Accessed August 6, 2024. https://corporatefinanceinstitute.com/resources/management/offshoring/.

Lotfi, Maryam and Abby Larmour. 2022. "Supply Chain Resilience in the Face of Uncertainty: How Horizontal and Vertical Collaboration can Help?" *Continuity & Resilience Review (Online)* 4(1): 37–53.

Maersk, 2021. "The Maersk Supply Chain Resilience Model—Preparing for and Managing Supply Chain Disruptions." *Maersk*. Assessed April 20, 2023. www.maersk.com/news/articles/2021/12/14/the-maersk-supply-chain-resilience-model.

Maharjan, Rajali and Hironori Kato. 2023. "Logistics and Supply Chain Resilience of Japanese Companies: Perspectives From Impacts of the COVID-19 Pandemic." *Logistics* 7(2): 27.

Malacina, Iryna and Roman Teplov. 2022. "Supply Chain Innovation Research: A Bibliometric Network Analysis and Literature Review." *International Journal of Production Economics* 251: 108540.

Mandal, Santanu and Rathin Sarathy. 2018. "The Effect of Supply Chain Relationships on Resilience: Empirical Evidence From India." *Global Business Review* 19 (3_suppl): S196–S217.

Marinagi, Catherine, Panagiotis Reklitis, Panagiotis Trivellas, and Damianos Sakas. 2023. "The Impact of Industry 4.0 Technologies on Key Performance Indicators for a Resilient Supply Chain 4.0." *Sustainability* 15(6): 5185

Martin, Christopher and Holweg. Matthias, 2011. ""Supply Chain 2.0": Managing Supply Chains in the Era of Turbulence." *International Journal of Physical Distribution & Logistics Management* 41(1): 63–82; Nakano,

Mikihisa. *Supply Chain Management Strategy and Organization*. Singapore: Springer, 2020.

McGrath A., Jonker A., 2023. "What Is Supply Chain Risk Management (SCRM)?" IBM.com. Accessed August 26, 2024. www.ibm.com/topics/supply-chain-risk-management.

McKinsey.com. 2023. "What Are Industry 4.0, the Fourth Industrial Revolution, and 4IR?. Accessed August 27, 2024. www.mckinsey.com/featured-insights/mckinsey-explainers/what-are-industry-4-0-the-fourth-industrial-revolution-and-4ir.

Mefford, R.N. 2009. "The Financial Crisis and Global Supply Chains." *AIB Insights* 9(3): 8–11.

Merino, Fernando, Cristina Di Stefano, and Luciano Fratocchi. 2021. "Back-Shoring Vs Near-Shoring: A Comparative Exploratory Study in the Footwear Industry." *Operations Management Research* 14(1–2): 17–37.

Michel-Villarreal, Rosario. 2023. "Towards Sustainable and Resilient Short Food Supply Chains: A Focus on Sustainability Practices and Resilience Capabilities Using Case Study." *British Food Journal (1966)* 125 (5): 1914–1935.

Microsoft.com. 2023. Upskilling vs. Reskilling: Similarities and Differences. < Upskilling vs. Reskilling: Similarities and Differences—Microsoft 365. Accessed August 8, 2024. www.microsoft.com/en-us/microsoft-365-life-hacks/organization/upskilling-vs-reskilling-similarities-and-differences?msoc kid=2dd872278e71642d03a3664c8f79654d.

Mills K.G., Reynolds E.B., Herculano M., 2022. Hbr.org. "Small Businesses Play a Big Role in Supply-Chain Resilience." Accessed August 27, 2024. https://hbr.org/2022/12/small-businesses-play-a-big-role-in-supply-chain-resilience.

MIT Centre for Transportation and Logistics. 2012. "Supply Chain Innovation: A Conceptual Framework. Accessed August 21, 2024. https://ctl.mit.edu/sites/ctl.mit.edu/files/MIT_SC_Innovation_Conceptual_Framework_Briefing.pdf.

Modgil, Sachin, Rohit Kumar Singh, and Claire Hannibal. 2022. "Artificial Intelligence for Supply Chain Resilience: Learning From Covid-19." *The International Journal of Logistics Management* 33(4): 1246–1268.

Mubarik, Muhammad Shujaat, Navaz Naghavi, Mobashar Mubarik, Simonov Kusi-Sarpong, Sharfuddin Ahmed Khan, Syed Imran Zaman, and Syed Hasnain Alam Kazmi. 2021. "Resilience and Cleaner Production in Industry 4.0: Role of Supply Chain Mapping and Visibility." *Journal of Cleaner Production* 292: 126058.

Muller, S. Raschid. 2022. "Analyzing Deficits in Awareness Among Chief Supply Chain Officers Who Have Not Adopted Cybersecurity as a Threat to Supply Chains."*IEEE*. doi:10.1109/ICMLANT56191.2022.9996456.

Munir, Muhammad Adeel, Amjad Hussain, Muhammad Farooq, Ateekh Ur Rehman, and Tariq Masood. 2024. "Building Resilient Supply Chains: Empirical Evidence on the Contributions of Ambidexterity, Risk Management, and Analytics Capability." *Technological Forecasting & Social Change* 200: 123146.

Munir, Manal, Muhammad Shakeel Sadiq Jajja, and Kamran Ali Chatha. 2022. "Capabilities for Enhancing Supply Chain Resilience and Responsiveness in the COVID-19 Pandemic: Exploring the Role of Improvisation, Anticipation, and Data Analytics Capabilities." *International Journal of Operations & Production Management* 42(10): 1576–1604.

Mwesiumo, Deodat, Bella B. Nujen, and Nina Pereira Kvadsheim. 2021. "A Systematic Approach to Implementing Multi-Sourcing Strategy in Engineer-to-Order Production." In *Advances in Production Management Systems. Artificial Intelligence for Sustainable and Resilient Production Systems*, A. Dolgui, A. Bernard, D. Lemoine, G. von Cieminski, A. Dolgui, D. Romero, A. Bernard, et al., eds, 633 vols, 381–389. Cham: Springer International Publishing.

Ndonye D.M., W.J.O. Odiyo, 2022. "Innovation and Supply Chain Resilience: A Theoretical Review." *Journal of Procurement & Supply Chain.* 6(1):106–126

Negri, Marta, Enrico Cagno, Claudia Colicchia, and Joseph Sarkis. 2021. "Integrating Sustainability and Resilience in the Supply Chain: A Systematic Literature Review and a Research Agenda." *Business Strategy and the Environment* 30(7): 2858–2886.

Newyorkfed.org. n.d. "Global Supply Chain Pressure Index (GSCPI)." Accessed August 26, 2024. www.newyorkfed.org/research/policy/gscpi#/overview.

Nguyen, Phu, Dmitry Ivanov, and Fabio Sgarbossa. 2023. "A Digital Twin–Based Approach to Reinforce Supply Chain Resilience: Simulation of Semiconductor Shortages." In *Advances in Production Management Systems. Production Management Systems for Responsible Manufacturing, Service, and Logistics Futures*, Erlend Alfnes, Anita Romsdal, Jan Ola Strandhagen, Gregor von Cieminski and David Romero, eds, 692 vols, 563–576. Cham: Springer Nature Switzerland.

Notteboom, T., T. Pallis, and J.P. Rodrigue. "Disruptions and Resilience in global container shipping and ports: the COVID-19 pandemic versus the 2008–2009 financial crisis." *Marit Econ Logist* 23: 179–210. https://doi.org/10.1057/s41278-020-00180-5.

Online.kettering.edu. 2016. "The Impact of Natural Disasters on Global Supply Chains. Accessed August 11, 2024. https://online.kettering.edu/news/impact-natural-disasters-global-supply-chains.

Ono, Takahiro, and Kenji Watanabe. 2015. "Application of Natural Disaster Information for Supply Chain Resilience." *Journal of Disaster Research* 10(sp): 783–786.

Oxfordreference.com. n.d. "Deagglomeration." Accessed August 28, 2024. www.oxfordreference.com/display/10.1093/oi/authority.20110803095 707477#:~:text=The%20movement%20of%20activity%2C%20 usually%20industry%2C%20away%20from,further%20agglomeration%20 in%20a%20region%20difficult%20and%20expensive.

Partanen, Jukka, Marko Kohtamäki, Pankaj C. Patel, and Vinit Parida. 2020. "Supply Chain Ambidexterity and Manufacturing SME Performance: The Moderating Roles of Network Capability and Strategic Information Flow." *International Journal of Production Economics* 221: 107470.

Paul, Sanjoy Kumar, Md Abdul Moktadir, and Kamrul Ahsan. 2023. "Key Supply Chain Strategies for the Post-COVID-19 Era: Implications for Resilience and Sustainability." *The International Journal of Logistics Management* 34(4): 1165–1187.

Piatanesi, Benedetta and Josep-Maria Arauzo-Carod. 2019. "Backshoring and Nearshoring: An Overview." *Growth and Change* 50(3): 806–823.

Pinho, T.M., A.P. Moreira, G.Veiga, and J. Boaventura-Cunha. 2015. "Overview of MPC Applications in Supply Chains: Potential Use and Benefits in the Management of Forest-Based Supply Chains." *Forest Systems* 24(3): e039–e039.

Pinho, Tatiana M., A. Paulo Moreira, Germano Veiga, and José Boaventura-Cunha. 2015. "Overview of MPC Applications in Supply Chains: Potential use and Benefits in the Management of Forest-Based Supply Chains." *Forest Systems* 24(3): e039–e039.

Piprani, Arsalan Zahid, Syed Abdul Rehman Khan, Rabiya Salim, and Muhammad Khalilur Rahman. 2023. "Unlocking Sustainable Supply Chain Performance Through Dynamic Data Analytics: A Multiple Mediation Model of Sustainable Innovation and Supply Chain Resilience." *Environmental Science and Pollution Research International* 30(39): 90615–90638.

Pnc.com. 2024. "Why Supply Chain Resilience Needs to Be a Top Priority in 2024." Accessed August 27, 2024. www.pnc.com/insights/small-business/ running-your-business/supply-chain-resilience-top-business-priority.html.

Pommeret, Aude, Francesco Ricci, and Katheline Schubert. 2022. "Critical Raw Materials for the Energy Transition." *European Economic Review* 141: 103991.

Power, Damien J., Amrik S. Sohal, and Shams-Ur Rahman. 2001. "Critical Success Factors in Agile Supply Chain Management—An Empirical Study." *International Journal of Physical Distribution & Logistics Management* 31(4): 247–265.

Pratono, Aluisius Hery, Ling Han, and Asri Maharani. 2023. "Global Supply Chain Resilience With the Flexible Partnership." *Modern Supply Chain Research and Applications* 5 (2): 102–114.

Pumilia, 2022 "What Is The Bullwhip Effect and How Can We Prevent It Next Time?" *Forbes.com*. Accessed August 15, 2024. www.forbes.com/councils/forbesbusinesscouncil/2022/04/07/what-is-the-bullwhip-effect-and-how-can-we-prevent-it-next-time/.

PwC.nl. 2022. "Increase in Risks Calls for More Resilient Supply Chains." Assessed April 20, 2023. www.pwc.nl/en/insights-and-publications/themes/economics/increase-in-risks-calls-for-more-resilient-supply-chains.html.

Qi, Yinan, Xiaorui Wang, Min Zhang, and Qiang Wang. 2023. "Developing Supply Chain Resilience Through Integration: An Empirical Study on an e-commerce Platform." *Journal of Operations Management* 69(3): 477–496.

Rajesh, R. 2017. "Technological Capabilities and Supply Chain Resilience of Firms: A Relational Analysis Using Total Interpretive Structural Modeling (TISM)." *Technological Forecasting & Social Change* 118: 161–169.

Rezaei, Ghazal, Seyed Mohammad Hassan Hosseini, and Shib Sankar Sana. 2022. "Exploring the Relationship Between Data Analytics Capability and Competitive Advantage: The Mediating Roles of Supply Chain Resilience and Organization Flexibility." *Sustainability* 14(16): 10444.

Rice J.B. Jr., Klibi W., Trepte K., 2022. "Overcoming the Financial Barriers to Building Resilient supply chains." *HBR.org*. Accessed August 26, 2024. https://hbr.org/2022/11/overcoming-the-financial-barriers-to-building-resilient-supply-chains.

Roostaie, S., N. Nawari, and C. J. Kibert. 2019. "Sustainability and Resilience: A Review of Definitions, Relationships, and their Integration into a Combined Building Assessment Framework." *Building and Environment* 154: 132–144.

Rui Ge and Hongmei Bao. 2024. "Digital Transformation and Resilience of Supply Chain in Manufacture Listed Firms: A Backward Spillover Effects in the Vertical Supply Chain Relationship." *Finance Research Letters* 65.

Sabahi, Sima and Mahour M. Parast. 2020. "Firm Innovation and Supply Chain Resilience: A Dynamic Capability Perspective." *International Journal of Logistics* 23(3): 254–269.

Safane, 2022. What Is the Global supply chain pressure index? A new tool that tracks how backed up supply chains are around the world. Accessed December 9, 2012. www.businessinsider.com/personal-finance#:~:text=The%20Global%20Supply%20Chain%20Pressure%20Index%20%28GSCPI%29%20is,those%20related%20to%20delivery%20times%2C%20prices%2C%20and%20inventory.

Sdgs.un.org. n.d. Natural Hazards, Unnatural Disasters. Accessed August 14, 2024. https://sdgs.un.org/publications/natural-hazards-unnatural-disasters-17250#:~:text=Earthquakes%2C%20droughts%2C%20floods%2C%20and%20storms%20are%20natural%20hazards%2C,result%20from%20human%20acts%20of%20omission%20and%20commission.

Sesana, Michele and Giacomo Tavola. 2021. "Resilient Manufacturing Systems Enabled by AI Support to AR Equipped Operator." *IEEE*. doi:10.1109/ICE/ITMC52061.2021.9570221.

Shan, Hongmei, Dongfang Bai, Xinmeng Fan, Jing Shi, Ying Li, and Shuhan Yang. 2023. "Enabling Roles of Integration and Resilience for Sustainable Supply Chain Performance: An Empirical Study on China's E-Commerce Platforms." *Applied Economics* 55(60): 7079–7093.

Sheffi Y. 2005. Building a Resilient Supply Chain. Accessed November 27, 2022. http://web.mit.edu/sheffi/www/selectedMedia/genmedia.buildingresilient supplychain.pdf.

Shen, Xin, Qianhui Xu, Qiao Liu, and Markus Leibercht. 2023. "The Relationship between Supply Chain Resilience, Supply Chain Integration, and Supply Chain Performance: A MASEM Analysis." *Journal of Intelligent & Fuzzy Systems* 45(2): 3361–3377.

Schuster R., G. Nath, P. Rodriguez, C. O' Brien, B. Aylor, B. Sidopoulos, D. Weise, et al. 2021. BCG.com. "Real World Supply Chain Resilience." Accessed August 26, 2024. www.bcg.com/publications/2021/building-resilience-strategies-to-improve-supply-chain-resilience.

Silva, Minelle E. and Salomée Ruel. 2022. "Inclusive Purchasing and Supply Chain Resilience Capabilities: Lessons for Social Sustainability." *Journal of Purchasing and Supply Management* 28(5): 100767.

Simchi -Levi David, Schnidt William, Wei Yehua, 2014. "From Superstorms to factory fires: Managing unpredictable supply chain disruptions." *Harvard Business Review*. Accessed December 21, 2022. https://hbr.org/2014/01/from-superstorms-to-factory-fires-managing-unpredictable-supply-chain-disruptions.

Singh, Nitya Prasad and Shubham Singh. 2019. "Building Supply Chain Risk Resilience: Role of Big Data Analytics in Supply Chain Disruption Mitigation." *Benchmarking : An International Journal* 26(7): 2318–2342.

Small business charter.org. 2024. "Supplier Diversity and Inclusive Supply Chains—A Call for Evidence. Accessed August 8, 2024. https://smallbusinesscharter.org/news-and-insights/news/supplier-diversity-and-inclusive-supply-chains-a-call-for-evidence.

Stark D. and O. Zweig. 2023. Ey.com. "Why Digital Supply Chain Visibility Should Be a Pharma Priority."" Accessed August 29, 2024. www.ey.com/en_uk/insights/life-sciences/digital-supply-chain-visibility-is-a-pharma-priority.

Stephens, Aaron Rae, Minhyo Kang, and Charles Arthur Robb. 2022. "Linking Supply Chain Disruption Orientation to Supply Chain Resilience and Market Performance with the Stimulus–Organism–Response Model." *Journal of Risk and Financial Management* 15(5): 227.

Stevens C. 2022. Business.org. "What Is Just-In-Time (JIT) Inventory Management?" Accessed August 26, 2024. www.business.org/finance/inventory-management/what-is-just-in-time-inventory-management/.

Stringer, Thomas and Monserrat Ramírez-Melgarejo. 2023. "Nearshoring to Mexico and US Supply Chain Resilience as a Response to the COVID-19 Pandemic." *Findings (Network Design Lab. Online).*

Supplychain247.com. "New Study Shows How Diversity and Inclusion Boost Supply Chain Success." Accessed August 27, 2024. www.supplychain247.com/article/new-study-shows-how-diversity-and-inclusion-boost-supply-chain-success.

Swink, Morgan, Igor Sant'Ana Gallo, Cliff Defee, and Andrea Lago Silva. 2024. "Supply Chain Visibility Types and Contextual Characteristics: A Literature-Based Synthesis." *Journal of Business Logistics* 45(1): n/a.

Tan, Hwee-Chin, Keng Lin Soh, Wai Peng Wong, and Ming-Lang Tseng. 2022. "Enhancing Supply Chain Resilience by Counteracting the Achilles Heel of Information Sharing." *Journal of Enterprise Information Management* 35(3): 817–846.

Tarafdar, Monideepa and Sufian Qrunfleh. 2017. "Agile Supply Chain Strategy and Supply Chain Performance: Complementary Roles of Supply Chain Practices and Information Systems Capability for Agility." *International Journal of Production Research* 55(4): 925–938.

Technologyreview.com. 2024. "Building Supply Chain Resilience With AI." Accessed August 27, 2024. www.technologyreview.com/2024/07/18/1094899/building-supply-chain-resilience-with-ai.

Tiwari, Manisha, David J. Bryde, Foteini Stavropoulou, Rameshwar Dubey, Sushma Kumari, and Cyril Foropon. 2024. "Modelling Supply Chain Visibility, Digital Technologies, Environmental Dynamism and Healthcare Supply Chain Resilience: An Organisation Information Processing Theory Perspective." *Transportation Research. Part E, Logistics and Transportation Review* 188: 103613.

Tradecouncil.org, 2022. "The Impact of Tariffs and Sanctions on International Trade" International Trade Council." Accessed August 18, 2024.

Trkman, Peter and Kevin McCormack. 2009. "Supply Chain Risk in Turbulent Raenvironments—A Conceptual Model for Managing Supply Chain Network Risk." *International Journal of Production Economics* 119(2): 247–258.

Trunk, Anna and Hendrik Birkel. 2022. "No Resilience Without Partners: A Case Study on German Small and Medium-Sized Enterprises in the Context of COVID-19." *Schmalenbach Journal of Business Research* 74(4): 537–574.

Umar, Muhammad and Mark Wilson. 2021. "Supply Chain Resilience: Unleashing the Power of Collaboration in Disaster Management." *Sustainability* 13(19): 10573.

Venkatarman, Anirudh and A. Dunstan Rajkumar. 2024. "Rajkumar and Venkataraman: Cross-Sectioning Sustainable Supply Chain Governance: A Bibliometric Analysis." *International Review of Management and Marketing* 14(3): 34–46.

Waredock.com. n.d. "Logistics Costs Explained." Accessed August 9, 2024. www.waredock.com/magazine/logistics-costs-explained/.

Waters, Donald. 2011. *Supply chain risk management: Vulnerability and Resilience in Logistics.* London: KoganPage.

Waters.J. n.d. Tive.com. "What Is OTIF, How to Calculate and How Did It Come About?" Accessed August 29, 2024. www.tive.com/blog/on-time-in-full-otif-what-is-otif-and-how-to-improve-metrics-with-technology.

Webb, J., 2017. "What Is the Kraljic Matrix?" *Forbes.com.* Accessed August 26, 2024. www.forbes.com/sites/jwebb/2017/02/28/what-is-the-kraljic-matrix/.

Weforum.org. 2022. "5 ways the COVID-19 pandemic has changed the supply chain. Accessed March 27, 2023. www.weforum.org/stories/2022/01/5-ways-the-covid-19-pandemic-has-changed-the-supply-chain/.

Wong, W.Y.C., Taih-Cherng Lirn, Ching-Chiao Yang, and Kuo-Chung Shang. 2020. "Supply Chain and External Conditions Under Which Supply Chain Resilience Pays: An Organizational Information Processing Theorization." *International Journal of Production Economics* 226: 107610.

Wu, Xia, Yang Li, and Zujun Zhu. 2023. "Does Online–Offline Channel Integration Matter for Supply Chain Resilience? The Moderating Role of Environmental Uncertainty." *Industrial Management + Data Systems* 123(5): 1496–1522.

Xia, Qing, Mengqi Quan, Haoran Li, and Xiaoru Hao. 2022. "Is Environmental Regulation Works on Improving Industrial Resilience of China? Learning From a Provincial Perspective." *Energy Reports* 8: 4695–4705.

Xu, Ting and Xinyu Liu. 2024. "Achieving Manufacturing Supply Chain Resilience: The Role of Paradoxical Leadership and Big Data Analytics Capability." *Journal of Manufacturing Technology Management* 35(2): 205–225.

Xu, Bowei, Weiting Liu, Junjun Li, Yongsheng Yang, Furong Wen, and Haitao Song. 2023. "Resilience Measurement and Dynamic Optimization of Container Logistics Supply Chain Under Adverse Events." *Computers & Industrial Engineering* 180: 109202.

Yuan, Yaqin and Wei Li. 2022. "The Effects of Supply Chain Risk Information Processing Capability and Supply Chain Finance on Supply Chain Resilience: A Moderated and Mediated Model." *Journal of Enterprise Information Management* 35(6): 1592–1612.

Yazdanparast, Reza, Reza Tavakkoli-Moghaddam, Razieh Heidari, and Leyla Aliabadi. 2021. "A Hybrid Z-Number Data Envelopment Analysis and

Neural Network for Assessment of Supply Chain Resilience: A Case Study." *Central European Journal of Operations Research* 29(2): 611–631.

Yossi H. 2007. "Building a Resilient Supply Chain." Hbr.org. Accessed August 20 2024. https://hbr.org/2007/08/building-a-resilient-supply-ch.

Young D., R. Hutchinson, M. Reeves. 2021. "The Green Economy Has a Resource-Scarcity Problem." Accessed April 20, 2023. https://hbr.org/2021/07/the-green-economy-has-a-resource-scarcity-problem.

Yu Han, Woon Kian Chong, and Dong Li. 2020. "A Systematic Literature Review of the Capabilities and Performance Metrics of Supply Chain Resilience." *International Journal of Production Research* 58(15): 4541–4566.

Zahidi S. 2020. "We need a global reskilling revolution—here's why' World Economic Forum." *World Economic Forum.* Accessed August 8, 2024. www.weforum.org/stories/2020/01/reskilling-revolution-jobs-future-skills/.

Zamani, Efpraxia D., Conn Smyth, Samrat Gupta, and Denis Dennehy. 2023. "Artificial Intelligence and Big Data Analytics for Supply Chain Resilience: A Systematic Literature Review." *Annals of Operations Research* 327(2): 605–632.

Zeng, Bingcong and Benjamin P. -C Yen. 2017. "Rethinking the Role of Partnerships in Global Supply Chains: A Risk-Based Perspective." *International Journal of Production Economics* 185: 52–62.

Zeplin Jiwa Husada Tarigan, Hotlan Siagian, and Jie Ferry. 2021. "Impact of Internal Integration, Supply Chain Partnership, Supply Chain Agility, and Supply Chain Resilience on Sustainable Advantage." *Sustainability* 13(10): 5460.

Zhou, Jinhua, Jianjun Zhu, and Hehua Wang. 2021. "Dual-Sourcing and Technology Cooperation Strategies for Developing Competitive Supplier in Complex Product Systems." *Computers & Industrial Engineering* 159: 107482.

Zhu, Stuart X. 2015. "Analysis of Dual Sourcing Strategies Under Supply Disruptions." *International Journal of Production Economics* 170: 191–203.

Zhuo, Ni, Chen Ji, and Nianchun Yin. 2021. "Supply Chain Integration and Resilience in China's Pig Sector: Case Study Evidences From Emerging Institutional Arrangements." *Environmental Science and Pollution Research International* 28 (7): 8310–8322.

About the Author

Andreas Karaoulanis is a professor of business and supply chain management with a long successful history in both industry and education. He is an accomplished researcher and an international author with several books on business management topics.

Index

OTHER TITLES IN THE SUPPLY AND OPERATIONS MANAGEMENT COLLECTION

Joy M. Field, Boston College, Editor

- *The Supply Chain Revolution* by Art Koch
- *The Warehouse Revolution* by Peter Devenyi, Miguel Pinilla and Jim Stollberg
- *An Introduction to Global Supply Chain Management* by Edmund Prater and Kim Whitehead
- *Transforming Quality Organizations* by Matthew P. Wictome and Ian Wells
- *Process Improvement to Company Enrichment* by Daniel Plung and Connie Krull
- *Organizational Velocity* by Alan Amling
- *C-O-S-T* by Craig Theisen
- *RFID for the Supply Chain and Operations Professional, Third Edition* by Pamela Zelbst and Victor Sower
- *Operations Management in China, Second Edition* by Craig Seidelson
- *Futureproofing Procurement* by Katie Jarvis-Grove
- *How Efficiency Changes* the Game by Ray Hodge
- *Supply Chain Planning, Second Edition* by Matthew J. Liberatore and Tan Miller
- *Sustainable Quality* by Joseph Diele

Concise and Applied Business Books

The Collection listed above is one of 30 business subject collections that Business Expert Press has grown to make BEP a premiere publisher of print and digital books. Our concise and applied books are for...

- Professionals and Practitioners
- Faculty who adopt our books for courses
- Librarians who know that BEP's Digital Libraries are a unique way to offer students ebooks to download, not restricted with any digital rights management
- Executive Training Course Leaders
- Business Seminar Organizers

Business Expert Press books are for anyone who needs to dig deeper on business ideas, goals, and solutions to everyday problems. Whether one print book, one ebook, or buying a digital library of 110 ebooks, we remain the affordable and smart way to be business smart. For more information, please visit www.businessexpertpress.com, or contact sales@businessexpertpress.com.

www.ingramcontent.com/pod-product-compliance
Lightning Source LLC
Chambersburg PA
CBHW061328220326
41599CB00026B/5091